HOW TO DRAFT ORDERS OF JUVENILE JUSTICE BOARD

A MANUAL FOR NON JUDICIAL OFFICERS

ATHOKPAM CHINGLEMBA LUWANG

ISBN
Hardcase 979-8-89777-694-8
Paperback 979-8-89744-624-7

Contents

Contents

Foreword 1

Keisam Pradipkumar
Hon'ble Chairperson,
Manipur Commission for
Protection of Child Rights

Address:
MCPCR, Directorate of
Social Welfare Building, 3rd
Floor, A.T. Line, Near 2nd
M.R. Gate, Imphal, Manipur
Pin-795001

A Good Law must be progressive in nature means it must be dynamic not static, evolving in align with the changing social values and necessities, effective with easy accessibility, ensuring fair and speedy justice, help bringing a just and vibrant society. Appropriate amendments or even repeals could be a part in its journey to fulfill desired goals for which the Law was enacted. In this context, the legislative history of juvenile justice laws in India testifies the same. The enactment of Juvenile Justice (Care & Protection of Children) Act, 2015 and subsequent amendments made up to 2021, underscored set of fundamental changes including a range of amendments, insertions, deletions, repealing, culminating the standards of UNCRC, broadening the power and functions of JJ bodies, providing JJ Act with overriding effects etc. Substituting old terms such as juvenile delinquents, neglected juveniles, juvenile home, arrest as used in 1986 version of JJ Act, by more courteous ones such as Juvenile in Conflict with Laws and later Child in Conflict with Law, Child in Need of Care and Protection, Children Home, apprehension etc. have significant impacts to change the attitudes towards child, childhood and juvenile justice system.

One shall be quite astounding to remember now, that a 'Juvenile'. as per JJ Act 1986 defined a boy who has not attained the age of sixteen years or a girl who has not attained the age of eighteen years. Ratifying the UNCRC in 1992 by India and enforcing a legal definition of Child i.e. "a child means any human being who has not attained the age of 18 years" (as per JJ Act 2000 and 2015) is path-breaking legislative reforms in the country. Besides, constitution of Juvenile Justice Committees headed by sitting judges in 2009 was another milestone which has conveniently brought juvenile justice laws and functioning under constant supervision of honorable judges, thereby making the juvenile justice bodies and state more accountable.

Why there are two terms "child" and "Juvenile" used in child laws, though the two words convey a similar meaning? The etymology of word Juvenile, a Latin term, derived from *juvenilis/juvenis* means young and young person, not different from the word "child". However, as a result of the way it has been desperately used, while describing a child having behavioral issues and committed an offence, in the laws and references; an implicit notion is being imbedded with the word "juvenile" and now it infers to describe a child who is allegedly committed an offence. In order to erase this perception, juvenile in conflict with Law which was mentioned in JJ Act 2000, was replaced by Child in Conflict with Law in JJ Act 2015. However, the journey has miles to go further.

The role of JJB becomes so crucial now than ever before. Under section 18 (3) of JJ Act 2015 allows the JJB to transfer a child's trial to a Children's court, if it decides that a trial is needed after a preliminary assessment. The JJB conducts preliminary assessment under Section 15 of the Act, where a CCL, between 16 years to 18 years of age, is alleged to have committed a heinous offence, to determine if the child should be tried as an adult or a child after considering the child's physical and mental capacity to commit the offence. In other word very fate of a CCL is being be decided by an Order of JJB. Here, having in-depth knowledge of JJ Act, proceedings of JJB and particularly acquiring drafting skills to pass appropriate Orders are absolutely necessary to become good and ideal JJB social worker members.

In this regard, Athokpam Chinglemba Luwang's manual entitled "How to Draft Orders of Juvenile Justice Board" is indeed a costly treasure not only for the sitting JJB Members but for all who have concerns for child rights. Since Manipur state has been exposed to protracted civil unrest and armed conflict situations dotted with lengthy bandhs, general strikes, blockades, agitations, many children have been affected in various ways. They have come out to streets as student protestors, sometimes at frontlines as village volunteers, sometimes as child soldiers. When such children are apprehended by police and produced before the JJBs, primary duties of the JJB is to pass appropriate Order in the best interest of the CCL, aiming to rehabilitation and social re-integration rather than punitive actions, guiding them to keep away from criminal activity in future. These objectives should be well reflected in subsequent Orders being issued.

The manual presented various relevant model Orders, based on the incidents often occurred in our society. Since the writer himself had earned long experience as a JJB member, the context and decisions taken are seemed to be quite practicable and relevant.

Lastly, let me reiterate the need for emphasizing General Principles of JJ Act, such as principle of presumption of innocence, principle of non-stigmatising semantics, principle of fresh start, principle of diversion, principle of non-wavering of rights, principle of best interest of CCL as far as possible. Essentially, children, including those who have allegedly committed offences, are the victims of the circumstances. We have to give proper treatment and improve the diseased circumstances (society), which are the breeding grounds of many wrong doing children, who do not know consequences for what they are doing. Therefore, indicators for successful functioning of JJBs should include the number of CCL cases transferred to the CWCs. I wish the users of the handbook get inspired mind with vital knowledge of laws, child rights and childhood, pure wisdom to issue just Orders.

With best Compliments

Date: 1ˢᵗ March 2025　　　　　　　　***Keisam Pradipkumar***
Chairperson
Manipur Commission for Protection of Child Rights

Foreword 2

Shri Salam Imocha Singh Address: Cheirap Court
Special Judge, Complex,
Fast Track Special Court Imphal, Manipur
No.1, Manipur Phone: 7005202962

J.J. Act has introduced a new jurisprudence for the Juvenile Justice System in the Criminal Justice System.

Under the Juvenile Justice System, decisions relating to the Children have always been taken on the basis of welfare and best interest of the child being regarded as paramount importance at every stage.

In this book, the author Shri Athokpam Chiglemba Luwang has provided important information regarding the various necessary and possible decisions/orders that may be taken/passed by the JJ Board in its proceeding under J.J. Act. The Author has in this book compiled various relevant orders which may be passed by the J.J. Board under J.J. Act regarding any circumstances that may arise for decision in the proceeding before it.

This book will be very helpful to those who are connected with the working of the J.J. Board and even others who wanted to know and learn about the working of the J.J. Board under the J.J. Act.

I congratulate the Author Shri Athokpam Chinglemba Luwang on his venture and recommend the book to all those dealing with the subject.

I wish the publication a grand success.

Date 24th February, 2025   **S. Imocha Singh**

Special Judge,
Fast Track Special Court No. 1, Manipur

Preface

I am deeply indebted to Shri Keisham Pradipkumar, the Hon'ble Chairperson of the Manipur Commission for Protection of Child Rights, and Shri Salam Imocha Singh, the Hon'ble Special Judge of Fast Track Special Court No. 1, Manipur, for their encouragement and forwarding this manual book.

Further, I received valuable assistance from my colleagues namely Smt. Takhelmayum Sunitibala and Smt. Ibemcha Ayekpam. Both of them are esteemed Members of the Juvenile Justice Boards of different districts of Manipur.

In this book, I am trying to present the ways of how a Social Worker Member having non-legal background education can draft an order effectively. For newly appointed Social Worker Members, understanding of the proceedings of the Board is a new lesson and drafting orders can be particularly a challenging task.

Social Worker Members of Boards hold the status of Non-Judicial Officers with first class magisterial powers. However, most Members come from non-legal background education. This book shall provide a clear and practical guide to help them draft orders efficiently and confidently.

Judicial writing is an art that requires logical reasoning, and I hope this book serves as a useful resource for them.

All the names mentioned in this book are fictitious and bear no relation to any real person. Similarly, FIR numbers and legal sections referenced are entirely fictional.

I am grateful to Notion Press for their invaluable support in making this book a grand success.

Athokpam Chinglemba Luwang
Date: 27 February 2025

Abbreviations and Acronyms

1. AMBA: All Manipur Bar Association
2. BNS: Bharatiya Nyaya Sanhita, 2023
3. BNSS: Bharatiya Nagarik Suraksha Sanhita 2023
4. CCL: Child in Conflict with Law
5. CJM: Chief Judicial Magistrate
6. C/D: Case Diary
7. CNCP: Child in Need of Care and Protection
8. CWPO: Child Welfare Police Officer
9. DeO: Data Entry Operator
10. DNA: Deoxyribonucleic acid
11. DoB: Date of Birth
12. FIR: First Information Report
13. FR: Filing Report
14. CR: Closing Report
15. i/c: in connection
16. I.E.: Imphal East
17. I.O.: Investigating Officer
18. IPC: India Penal Code
19. JJB/ JJ Board: Juvenile Justice Board
20. JJ Act/ JJ Act 2015: Juvenile Justice (Care and Protection of Children) Act, 2015
21. JJ Rules 2016: Juvenile Justice (Care and Protection of Children) Model Rules, 2016

22. JMFC: Judicial Magistrate First Class
23. Ld.: Learned
24. LPO: Legal Cum Probation Officer
25. OC: Officer-in-Charge
26. PO: Post Office
27. PS: Police Station
28. PW: prosecution witness
29. SBR: Social Background Report
30. S.I.: Sub Inspector
31. SIR: Social Investigation Report
32. SJPU: Special Juvenile Police Unit
33. SPT: Senapati
34. TIP: Test Identification Parade
35. U/S: under section
36. WPS: Women Police Station

PART 1

Introduction

This manual book aims to provide a simple and practical guide to drafting orders for Social Worker Members especially those from non-legal backgrounds.

I offer some key suggestions for them. Upon appointment as a Member, it is essential to study case files and review how the previous orders have been written. Additionally, a Member should seek guidance from Principal Magistrate when in doubt and learn from senior Members. A thorough understanding of the Juvenile Justice (JJ) Act and Rules, Bharatiya Sakshya Adhiniyam 2023, Bharatiya Nagarik Suraksha Sanhita 2023 and Bharatiya Nyaya Sanhita 2023 is crucial.

A Juvenile Justice Board (JJB) is a non-criminal court that deals with children in conflict with the law/children who are alleged to have committed an offence. As a Member, it is essential to be familiar with the key provisions of Criminal Procedure Code, 1973 (now Bharatiya Nagarik Suraksha Sanhita 2023), JJ Act and Rules. The proceedings must be conducted in accordance with these laws. Additionally, international covenants such as Convention on the Rights of the Child, the United Nations Standard Minimum Rules for the Administration of Juvenile Justice, 1985 (the Beijing Rules), the United Nations Rules for the Protection of Juveniles Deprived of their Liberty (1990) should be kept in mind.

In practice, it is important to develop a working knowledge of these laws. Many Members may initially feel hesitant about understanding legal procedures, but one of their responsibilities is to provide opinions on non-legal matters. This is precisely why professionals from diverse educational backgrounds are included in the board. Members should take pride in having different stream of education other than legal schooling.

One of the primary duties of a Member is to give opinions in the best interest of the child. These opinions may be expressed during discussions, incorporated into orders or presented as dissenting opinions. Dissenting opinion is an opinion of one or more juries which disagree with the reasoning stated in the majority in a bench. In the Board, it is a formal disagreement with the majority decision. Dissenting opinions shall be better if it is put up in a written manner. For these reasons, the skill of drafting orders is essential part of a Member's role.

Before learning how to draft orders, it is important to understand procedural steps involved in handling a case before the Board. The following table provides a concise overview of these steps.

STEPS OF PROCEEDING

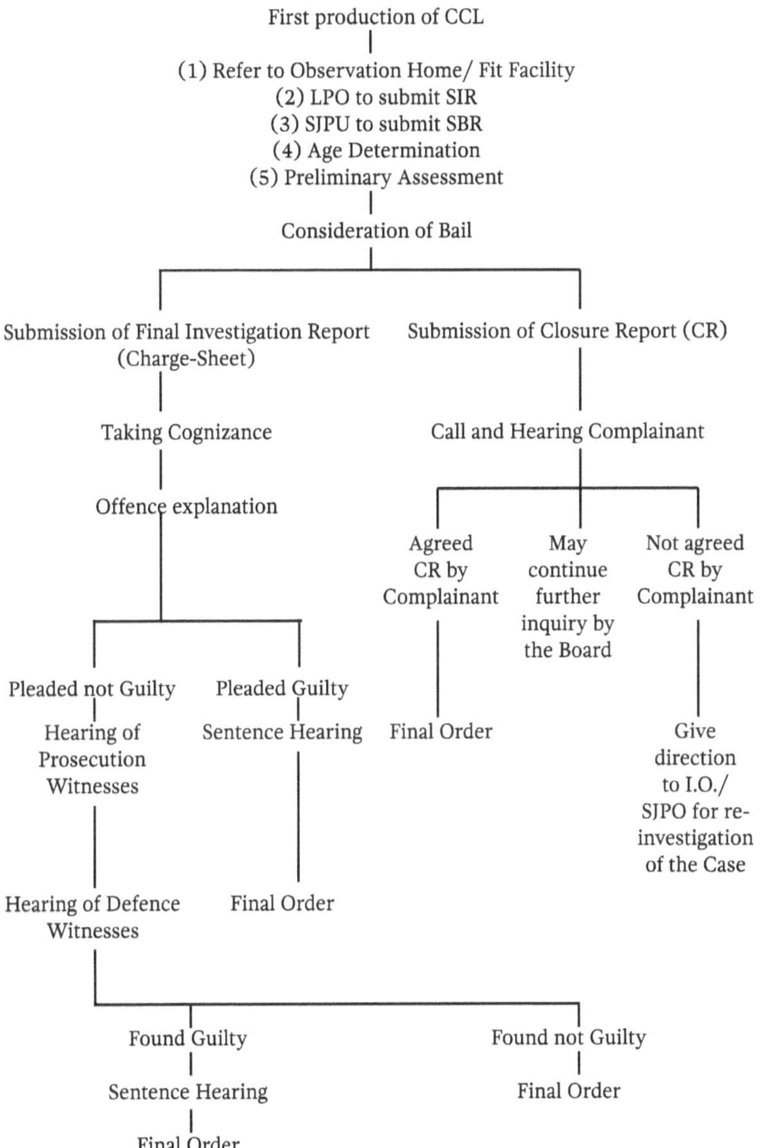

Components of an Order

When drafting an order, please omit words which may infer derogatory connotations to child and childhood. We shall use the word 'offence' instead of 'crime'. *"Principle of non-stigmatizing semantics suggests not to use words which are used in normal criminal proceedings, decisions and actions that might stigmatize the juveniles. The principle mandates to avoid the use of adversarial or accusatory words, such as, arrest, remand, accused, charge sheet, trial, prosecution, warrant, summons, conviction, inmate, delinquent, neglected, custody or jail. This principle expects not to use these words, but it does not mention the substitutes of the terms except some words, viz., Child in Conflict with Law (CCL) for Accused, apprehended for arrested, inquiry for trial.*[1]

There is no hard and fast rule of writing an order. However, there are some basic ideas which can be kept in mind employed in the order. *"Writing of judgments and orders is virtually an art which often varies from judge to judge as on form of format has been provided in law as to what should be written in a judgment or order and what should not.*[2]

Key Components of an Order

When drafting an order, the following essential components should be considered:

---

[1] *Rights of Juveniles*, Athokpam Chinglemba Luwang, 2019

[2] An essay on *How to write Judgment and Orders* by S. S. Upadhya, Former District & Session Judge/ Former Legal Advisor to the Governor of Utter Pradesh.

i. **Facts and circumstances**: Clearly state the facts and circumstances related to the commission of the offence.

ii. **Records**: It should be perused the records on material available in the case file of the Board.

iii. **Appraisal of evidence**: Oral or documentary evidence including electronic records should be quoted and analytically appreciated in orders which is really needed for deciding the rights.

iv. **Law and Ruling**: The provision of the law related with case must be quoted and analyzed. Non mentioning of the provision under which the power was exercised in passing orders shall deprive of efficacy of the orders.

v. **Simple language**: Use clear and concise language to ensure the order effectively communicates the liabilities of the parties and the key issues in the case.

vi. **Avoid use of ambiguous or confused words**: Ensure clarity by avoiding vague or misleading terms.

vii. **Avoid lengthy sentences**: Lengthy sentences should be avoided as to deter from confusion and mistake.

viii. **Use of legal terms**: Always use prescribed legal terms. If not available such words, then words and phraseology used by the parties and the lawyers may be used.

ix. **Avoid proverbs and phrases**: Use of proverbs, phrases, idioms, ornamental words should be avoided.

x. **Use distinct paragraphs**: Paragraphs should be divided to record different parts of the order.

xi. **Inclusion of arguments**: Real part of the arguments of the both parties must be quoted. It is not necessary to quote all the arguments.

xii.   **Avoid subjectivity:** Members should avoid sentimental opinion, subjective view, individual philosophy, imaginary or fanciful ideas.

By adhering to these guidelines, Social Worker Members can ensure that their orders are structured, logical, and legally sound, while maintaining the best interests of the child as primary focus.

Roles of Members

Principal Magistrates are legally qualified professionals trained to handle critical cases. In contrast, Social Worker Members do not receive extensive legal training. Therefore, in cases involving complex legal issues, Members should rely on the Principal Magistrate for guidance.

It is good if a Social Worker Member is well-versed in drafting Orders and procedures, still one should not lose heart because of lack of proficiency in this field. Their tenure is temporary, lasting for three years, with the possibility of reappointment for another term. In some Indian states, a member may serve under non ordinary conditions beyond two terms, e.g., Mizoram.

Drafting Orders on First Production of a Child in Conflict with Law (CCL)

Section 7(2) of the JJ Act, 2015 mentions that *"A child in conflict with law may be produced before an individual member of the Board when the Board is not in sitting."*

This means that Members must be familiar with drafting an order when a CCL is first presented before them in the absence of a full Board sitting. To assist with this, a specimen order is provided in this book, which can be memorized or used as a reference model.

Preliminary Assessment under Section 15 of the JJ Act, 2015: Another critical responsibility of a Member is conducting a preliminary assessment as per Section 15 of the JJ Act, 2015. The provision states:

"In case of a heinous offence alleged to have been committed by a child, who has completed or is above the age of sixteen years, the Board shall conduct a preliminary assessment with regard to his mental and physical capacity to commit such offence, ability to understand the consequences of the offence and the circumstances in which he allegedly committed the offence, and may pass an order in accordance with the provisions of subsection (3) of section 18:

Provided that for such an assessment, the Board may take the assistance of experienced psychologists or psycho-social workers or other experts."

When a CCL above the age of 16 years is alleged of committing a heinous offence, the Board must conduct a preliminary assessment to determine:

- The child's mental and physical capacity to commit the offence
- Their ability to understand the consequences of the offence
- The circumstances under which the offence was allegedly committed

This assessment is crucial in deciding whether the child should be tried as an adult or not. Therefore, the opinions of Members hold significant weight in this process. This book provides guidelines and specimen orders to assist Members in drafting such assessments.

Members' Role in Ensuring the Welfare of Children

Beyond legal responsibilities, Members play a vital role in safeguarding the overall development and welfare of juveniles, adhering to the *Principle of the Best Interest of the Child*. This includes ensuring the child's education, health & nutrition, vocational training, leisure & recreational activities etc. To fulfill these responsibilities, Members are required to express their opinions on these matters in the form of orders.

PART 2

First Production of a Child in Conflict with Law (CCL)

A Child in Conflict with Law (CCL) must be produced before the JJB or an individual Member within twenty-four (24) hours from the time of apprehension. Odd hours (such as late nights, travel time) are not counted in this timeframe.

Key Considerations at First Production

At the first production, the Board must check the following conditions:

i. **Physical or Mental Assault** – Ensure the child has not been harmed by the police or any other person.
ii. **Handcuffing** – If the CCL is handcuffed, advise the police accordingly.
iii. **Hunger & Starvation** – If the child is hungry, provide food.
iv. **Inappropriate Clothing** – If the clothes are not suited to the weather, arrange for proper clothing.
v. **Substance Abuse** – If the child appears to be a drug addict, direct them to keep at a fit facility or an approved rehabilitation centre.

vi. **Mental Health Concerns** – If the child appears mentally unwell, arrange for admission to a fit facility or refer to the concerned department.

vii. **Medical Conditions** – If the child has HIV, Hepatitis, or any other diseases, refer them to an appropriate medical facility.

viii. **Physical Disabilities** – If the child has a disability, ensure they receive necessary support services at a fit facility or approved centre.

ix. **Any Other Considerations** – The Board may check additional conditions as deemed necessary.

Essential Documents to Check at First Production

The Board must verify the following documents:

i. Age proof documents /certificates;
ii. FIR copy;
iii. Forwarding copy submitted by I.O./SJPU/CWPO;
iv. Social Background Report (SBR);
v. Medical check-up report;
vi. Seizure report, etc.

Tips for drafting an Order on First Production of a CCL

Before drafting the order, keep the following points in mind:

i. **Title of order:** Write the word "Order" at the centre of the upper part of the paper;
ii. **Date of order:** mention the date below the title;
iii. **Basic details of CCL:** include the name and address, age of the CCL.

iv. **Prosecution history**: provide brief background of the case;

v. **Date of Birth**: Record date of birth or age of the CCL;

vi. **Free Legal Aid**: Mention the provision of Free Legal Aid for the child if required;

vii. **Parental notification**: Mention to inform the parents/guardians and present before the board at the next sitting;[3]

viii. **Social Background Report (SBR)**: Mention of Social Background Report (SBR) which is to be submitted by I.O./SJPU; if not submitted, please give directive them to submit the same on or before the next sitting;

ix. **Questioning of the CCL**: Order may be given for taking interview or questioning the CCL by the SJPU in the presence of the Superintendent of the Home (Child Care Institution).

x. **Social Investigation Report**: Give directive to LPO for submitting SIR within 15 days from the date of the order.

xi. **Next sitting date**: fix a date for the next sitting

xii. **Signatures:** A Member or Principal Magistrate or both or all the three juries must sign the order

---

3   under section13 (i), JJ Act 2015

A specimen order of Production of CCL

Ref: FIR: 21 (7) 2024 SPT PS

U/S 64 BNS

<u>ORDER</u>

14/7/2024

The CCL namely Narayan Singh, 16 yrs, s/o Harideva Singh of Taranithoi Bazar, PO & PS Senapati, Senapati District is produced before the board. The prosecution history is that the CCL had stolen a car from the Garage of Shri.... from.... (address) in the night of 12/3/2024. He was apprehended on 13/7/0224 at around 6 p.m. from his house.

The date of birth of the CCL is 15 days 4 months and 17 years as per record of matriculation certificate.

The CCL shall be provided free legal aid if their parents or guardians have no capacity to engage private lawyers.

The Legal-cum-Probation officer is directed to submit SIR (Social Investigation Report) within 15 days from the date of this order.

CWPO (I.O.) is directed to inform the parents or guardians of the CCL to present at the next sitting.

CWPO is further directed to submit SBR on or before the next sitting.

The investigation is at an early stage, it is required further enquiry. So, CCL is referred to the Observation Home. The Superintendent of Observation Home is directed to receive the CCL and keep CCL at the safe custody and shall be produced before the Board on 24/3/2024. During the stay at the Observation Home, the CWPO shall take interview in the presence of Superintendent of the Home.

Fixed 24/7/2024 for the production of the CCL.

(signature)   (signature)

Member   Member

Juvenile Justice Board   Juvenile Justice Board

Senapati District   Senapati District

Referring To Observation Home

As per Rule no. 9(2) of JJ Rules, the CCL may be kept at the Observation Home by using Form 4 of JJ Rules. A Specimen Order to refer the CCL to Observation Home is given below:

Before the Juvenile Justice Board,

Senapati District, Manipur

JJB/SPT Case No. 6 of 2024

Ref: FIR No. 21(07)2024 SPT PS, u/s 64 BNS

The State of Manipur

Vs

Narayan Singh, 17 yrs

s/o Harideva Singh

Taranithoi Bazar,

PO & PS Senapati, Senapati District, Manipur

To,

The Superintendent

Observation Home,

Takyel.

Whereas on 13th July 2024, CCL namely Narayan Singh, 16 yrs, s/o Harideva Singh of Taranithoi Bazar, PO & PS Senapati, Senapati District is ordered by Board to be kept in the Observation Home for a period of ten days

This is authorized and required you to receive the said CCL into your charge, and to keep him in the Observation Home and to produce the CCL as and when directed by the Board, for the aforesaid order to be carried into execution according to law.

Next date of sitting: 23/07/2024.

Given my hand and seal of Juvenile Justice Board.

Senapati/Dated 13/7/2024.

(Signature)
Member
Juvenile Justice Board
Senapati District.

PART 3

Age Determination of a Child in Conflict with Law (CCL)

General Principle of Age Determination

The age of a CCL may be determined based on the appearance or prima facie unless there is differing opinions. If there is doubt based on the appearance, academic credentials should be considered. Where academic credentials are not available, birth certificates given by a corporation or a municipal authority or a panchayat should be considered.

Only in the absence of the above documents or conditions, age shall be determined by ossification test or any other latest medical age determination test.

Favouring the Juvenile in Borderline Cases

In the matter of petty cases, if there are two or more views or conflicting documents mentioning different ages for a juvenile, the JJB must take a child-friendly approach and lean in favour of juvenility.

While dealing with question of determination of the age of the accused for the purpose finding out whether he is juvenile or not, a hyper-technical approach should not be adopted while appreciating the evidence adduced on behalf of the accused in support of the plea that he is a juvenile and if two views may be possible on the said evidence the court should lean in favour of holding the accused to be a juvenile in border line cases; *Arnith Das versus State of Bihar reported in 2000 Legal Eagle (SC) 970.*[4]

Prima Facie Determination of Age

In the cases of petty offence, the Board may record the age of the CCL based on appearance or prima facie when there is doubt or different opinions.

Where, it is obvious to the Committee or the Board, based on the appearance of the person brought before it under any of the provisions of this Act (other than for the purpose of giving evidence) that the said person is a child, the Committee or the Board shall record such observation stating the age of the child as nearly as may be...[5]

It is no doubt true that if there is a clear and unambiguous case in favour of the juvenile accused that he was a minor below the age of 18 years on the date of the incident and the documentary evidence at least *prima facie* proves the same, he would be entitled to the special protection under the JJ Act; *Parag Bhati (Juvenile).... Appellant(s) through. Legal Guardian-Mother-Smt. Rajni Bhati Versus State of Uttar Pradesh and Anr... Respondent(s), CRIMINAL APPEAL NO. 486 OF 2016, SC.*[6]

---

4   Arnith Das versus State of Bihar reported in 2000 Legal Eagle (SC) 970

5   Section 94. (1) JJ Act 2015

6   Parag Bhati (Juvenile).... Appellant(s) through. Legal Guardian-Mother-Smt. Rajni Bhati Versus State of Uttar Pradesh and Anr..... Respondent(s), CRIMINAL APPEAL NO. 486 OF 2016, SC

School Certificates and Academic Records in Age Determination

The date of birth certificate from the school, or the matriculation or equivalent certificate from the concerned examination Board should be given preference in determination of age.[7]

We are of the view that admission register in the school in which the candidate first attended is a relevant piece of evidence of the date of birth. The reasoning that the parents could have entered a wrong date of birth in the admission register hence date of birth is equal to thinking that parents would do so in anticipation that child would commit a crime in future and, in that situation, they could successfully raise a claim of juvenility; *Ashwini Kumar Saxena V. State of M.P.,2012; Criminal Appeal No. 1403 of 2012, Special Leave Petition (Crl) No. 7271 of 2021, SC.*[8]

It is a settled position of law that if the matriculation or equivalent certificates are available and there is no other material to prove the correctness, the date of birth mentioned in the matriculation certificate has to be treated as a conclusive proof of the date of birth of the accused; *Parag Bhati (Juvenile).... Appellant(s) through. Legal Guardian-Mother-Smt. Rajni Bhati Versus State of Uttar Pradesh and Anr... Respondent(s), CRIMINAL APPEAL NO. 486 OF 2016, SC.*[9]

---

7   Section 94(2)(i) of JJ Act 2015

8   Ashwini Kuamr Saxena V.State of M.P.,2012; Criminal Appeal No. 1403 of 2012, Special Leave Petition (Crl) No. 7271 of 2021, SC

9   Parag Bhati (Juvenile).... Appellant(s) through. Legal Guardian-Mother-Smt. Rajni Bhati Versus State of Uttar Pradesh and Anr..... Respondent(s), CRIMINAL APPEAL NO. 486 OF 2016, SC

Doubt over the Matriculation or Academic Certificates & Ossification Test

When to Conduct an Ossification Test;

As per the Juvenile Justice (JJ) Act, 2015, ossification test or latest medical age determination test shall be performed only when the academic age proof certificates or birth certificate given by a corporation or municipal authority or panchayat are not available.

However, despite these proviso-guidelines, practical challenges may arise in determining a child's age, such as:

1. Discrepancies between the date of birth recorded at the time of school admission and that mentioned in the matriculation certificate.
2. Changes in age records when a child transfers to a different school.
3. Two different matriculation certificates indicating different ages. A similar issue was encountered in Juvenile Justice Board, Imphal East District (2016).[10]
4. Contradictory age records across official documents such as:

   - Aadhar Card
   - Voter Card
   - Matriculation Certificate
   - Self-testimony of the CCL

It is a settled position of law that if the matriculation or equivalent certificates are available and there is no other

---

10 It was found that a CCL appeared two different metric exams at CBSE and Manipur Board recording different ages

material to prove the correctness, the date of birth mentioned in the matriculation certificate has to be treated as a conclusive proof of the date of birth of the accused. However, if there is any doubt or a contradictory stand is being taken by the accused which raises a doubt on the correctness of the date of birth then as laid down by this Court in **Abuzar Hossain (supra)**, an enquiry for determination of the age of the accused is permissible which has been done in the present case; *Parag Bhati (Juvenile).... Appellant(s) through. Legal Guardian-Mother-Smt. Rajni Bhati Versus State of Uttar Pradesh and Anr... Respondent(s), CRIMINAL APPEAL NO. 486 OF 2016, SC.*[11]

It is no doubt true that if there is a clear and unambiguous case in favour of the juvenile accused that he was a minor below the age of 18 years on the date of the incident and the documentary evidence at least *prima facie* proves the same, he would be entitled to the special protection under the JJ Act. But when an accused commits a grave and heinous offence and thereafter attempts to take statutory shelter under the guise of being a minor, a casual or cavalier approach while recording as to whether an accused is a juvenile or not cannot be permitted as the courts are enjoined upon to perform their duties with the object of protecting the confidence of common man in the institution entrusted with the administration of justice; *Parag Bhati (Juvenile).... Appellant(s) through. Legal Guardian-Mother-Smt. Rajni Bhati Versus State of Uttar*

---

11 Parag Bhati (Juvenile).... Appellant(s) through. Legal Guardian-Mother-Smt. Rajni Bhati Versus State of Uttar Pradesh and Anr..... Respondent(s), CRIMINAL APPEAL NO. 486 OF 2016, SC

Pradesh and Anr... Respondent(s), CRIMINAL APPEAL NO. 486 OF 2016, SC.[12]

When there is reasonable doubt over the age recorded in the certificates of a CCL who has committed a heinous offence, performing a medical test or ossification test shall be a right approach. The Board must be sensitive in dealing with juveniles who have committed serious and heinous offences.

When a Medical Test is Necessary

The juvenile who is involved in cases of serious offence like sexual molestation, rape, gang rape, murder and host of other offences, the accused cannot be allowed to abuse the statutory protection by attempting to prove himself as a minor when the documentary evidence to prove his minority gives rise to a reasonable doubt about his assertion of minority; *Om Prakash vs. State of Rajasthan and Another (2012) 5 SCC 201.*[13]

Thus, when there is **reasonable doubt** over a juvenile's **age in a serious or heinous offence,** an **ossification test or latest medical age determination test** may be conducted.

---

12 Parag Bhati (Juvenile).... Appellant(s) through. Legal Guardian-Mother-Smt. Rajni Bhati Versus State of Uttar Pradesh and Anr..... Respondent(s), CRIMINAL APPEAL NO. 486 OF 2016, SC

13 Om Prakash vs. State of Rajasthan and Another (2012) 5 SCC 201

PART 4

Recording of Photograph and Fingerprint

In our view, therefore, it is open to the investigating agency to utilize minimum possible time to interrogate the accused and to take his identification marks, finger prints, photographs, etc., which would help the police not only to bring the arrested person to book, but also furnish clue or linkage of the offence with other offenders and offences; *Pravinkumar Chandrakant Vyas and Anr. Vs. State of Gujarat and Ors, 2021 Gujarat High Court.*[14]

Specimen order of allowing finger prints and photographs

Before the Juvenile Justice Board

Senapati District

JJB/SPT Misc Case No. 22 of 2024

Ref No. FIR No. 11(8)2024 SPT PS

u/s 118(2)/103 BNS

---

14 Pravinkumar Chandrakant Vyas and Anr. Vs. State of Gujarat and Ors, 2021 Gujarat High Court

The State of Manipur

Vs

Narayan Singh, 16 yrs

s/o Harideva Singh

Taranithoi Bazar,

PO & PS Senapati, Senapati District, Manipur

<u>ORDER</u>

25/08/2024

The application is submitted by the CWPO /I.O. of the case praying the Board to allow the recording of Photograph and fingerprint of the CCL for smooth investigation of the case.

Registered it as the JJB Misc. Case No 22 of 2024.

Brief fact of the case is that on 2/8/2024 at about 1;30 p.m. Sudhir's mother namely Panchashila aged 75 yrs old of Taoroinai bazaar, Senapati was found injured and unconscious, suspected to have been assaulted by an unknown miscreant at the jungle about 3 kms. from the northern side of Taoroinai Bazar. The victim was first evacuated to District Hospital on the same day for further treatment. The victim succumbed to injuries at the Hospital. Hectic efforts were made to identify the culprits who committed the crime by engaging private sources. On 6/8/2024 at about 10:30 a.m., a team of Senapati PS went to Taoroinai Bazar and apprehended a CCL namely Narayan Singh aged about 16 years. One khukri was seized from the juvenile.

Perused the records on materials, considered the intensity of the offence and the rights of the CCL.

For the interest of Justice, the prayer is allowed.

The CWPO/I.O. is directed to conduct the procedure under a child friendly atmosphere.

The Superintendent of Observation Home, Takyelpat, Social Welfare Department is directed to cooperate with the CWPO/IO of the case by allowing CCL to take photographs and fingerprint of the CCL at the concerned office.

Send copies of this order to CWPO and the Superintendent of Observation Home, Takyelpat.

The Misc case is disposed of accordingly.

(signature)   **(signature)**
Member   Member
Juvenile Justice Board   Juvenile Justice Board
Senapati District   Senapati District

PART 5

DNA Profiling

DNA (Deoxyribonucleic acid) is the genetic blue print for life and is found specially in cell nuclei which are the foundation of heredity. Blood grouping test is a perfect test to determine questions of disputed paternity of a child and can be relied upon by courts as a circumstantial evidence which excludes a certain individual as a father of the child; *Gautam Kundu v. State of West Bengal, 1993 Cr LJ3233 (SC): (1993)3 SCC 418: AIR 1993 SC 2295.*[15]

DNA profiling can be scientific evidence to prove the accused involved in the rape cases.

Specimen order of DNA Profiling

Before the Juvenile Justice Board,
Senapati East, Manipur

Reference: 15(9)2024 SPT PS
u/s 70(D)/3(5) BNS & sec 6 POCSO Act '12

JJB Misc. Case No. 11 of 2024
State

---

15 Gautam Kundu v. State of West Bengal, 1993 Cr LJ3233 (SC): (1993)3 SCC 418: AIR 1993 SC 2295

Vs

1. Narayan Singh, 16 yrs, s/o Harideva Singh, Taranithoi Bazar, PO & PS Senapati, Senapati District, Manipur.
2. David Panmei. 16 yrs, s/o Kakhuran Panmei, Taranithoi Bazar, PO & PS Senapati, Senapati District, Manipur.
3. Lorii Dikho, s/o Puni Dikho, Taranithoi Bazar, PO & PS Senapati, Senapati District, Manipur.

.....Children in Conflict with Law

<u>ORDER</u>

20/9/2024

1. The present petition is filed by the SJPO/ WPS-IE who is investigating the above mentioned FIR for allowing to conduct DNA profiling test.
2. Registered it JJB Misc Case No. 11 of 2024.
3. The brief facts of the case is that on 17th Augustr 2024 at 6.10 p.m., OC Women PS, Senapati received a written report submitted by Kaikhro of Senapati stating that on 14th August 2024, at about 10:10 -11 P.m., three CCLs forcibly gang raped a minor girl at a corner of Senapati foothill.
4. It is stated some items containing seminal stains/ pubic hair/ hairs were seized during the investigation of the case and it is required to collect samples from the victims and CCLs for the purpose of investigation.
5. Perused the record and heard the petitioner. The DNA samples are required for the purpose of establishing

identity of the persons involved and for the purpose of investigation. The prayer for collection of DNA samples is allowed. The samples are to be collected by following the due procedure of law.

6. Application is allowed and disposed of.

(**signature**)   (**signature**)

Member   Member

Juvenile Justice Board   Juvenile Justice Board

Senapati District   Senapati District

PART 6

Test Identification Parade (TIP)

The idea of holding Test Identification Parade under section 9 of evidence Act is to test the veracity of the witness on the question of his capacity to identify an unknown person whom the witness may have seen only once. It on T.I.P is held then it will be wholly unsafe to rely on his bare testimony regarding the identification of an accused for the first-time in court; *Kanan v. State of Kerala, AIR 1979 SC 1127; 1979 SCC (Cri) 621: (1979) 3 SCC 391.*[16]

The purpose of a prior test identification is to test and strengthen the trustworthiness of evidence of identification of the accused person at the trial. The evidence of mere identification of the accused person at the trial for the first time is from its very nature inherently of a weak character. It is accordingly considered a safe rule of prudence to generally look for corroboration of the sworn testimony of witnesses in court as to the identity of the accused who are strangers to them, in the form of earlier identification proceedings; *Munshi Singh Gautam v. State of Madhya Pradesh, (2005) 9 SCC 631.*[17]

---

16 Kanan v. State of Kerala, AIR 1979 SC 1127; 1979 SCC (Cri) 621: (1979) 3 SCC 391
17 Munshi Singh Gautam v. State of Madhya Pradesh, (2005) 9 SCC 631

Specimen order of TIP

Before the Juvenile Justice Board,
Senapati East, Manipur

Reference: 15(9)2024 SPT/WPS PS
u/s 70(2)//3(5) BNS & sec 6 POCSO Act '12

JJB Misc. Case No. 17 of 2024
State
Vs

1. Narayan Singh, 16 yrs, s/o Harideva Singh, Taranithoi Bazar, PO & PS Senapati, Senapati District, Manipur.
2. David Panmei. 16 yrs, s/o Kakhuran Panmei, Taranithoi Bazar, PO & PS Senapati, Senapati District, Manipur.
3. Lorii Dikho, s/o Puni Dikho, Taranithoi Bazar, PO & PS Senapati, Senapati District, Manipur.

...Children in Conflict with Law

ORDER
29/9/2024

Application filed by the SJPU SPT/WPS Mrs. Lucy Kamei, praying to be allowed to conduct TIP (Test Identification Parade) of the CCLs during their stay at the Observation Home i/c with the above mentioned FIR.

Registered it JJB Misc Case No. 17 of 2024.

The brief facts of the case is that on 17th September 2024 at 6.10 p.m., OC Women PS, Senapati received a written report submitted by Kaikhro of Senapati stating that on 14th

September 2024, at about 10:10 -11 P.m., three CCLs forcibly gang raped a minor girl at a corner of Senapati foothill.

It is prayed that the invariably requirement to conduct TIP since the victim girl needs to establish the identity of the perpetrators as per law.

The Board is in the opinion to accept the application as to establish the facts and circumstances.

So, the prayer is allowed

Disposed of this misc. case accordingly.

(Signature)	**(Signature)**
Member	Member
Juvenile Justice Board	Juvenile Justice Board
Senapati District	Senapati District

PART 7

Recording the Statement of Raped Victim

Every child shall have a right to protect of their privacy and confidentiality, by all means and throughout the judicial process. No report of the rape victim shall be published in newspapers and media which leads to the identification of the victim.

The right to privacy is implicit in the right to life and liberty guaranteed to the citizens of this country by Article 21; *R. Rajgopal vs State of T.N. on 7 October 1994, Supreme Court of India.*[18]

Section 25 of Protection of Children from Sexual Offences Act, 2012 states that:

Recording of statement of a child by Magistrate — (1) If the statement of the child is being recorded under section 164 of the Code of Criminal Procedure, 1973 (2 of 1974) (herein referred to as the Code), the Magistrate recording such statement shall, notwithstanding anything contained therein, record the statement as spoken by the child:

---

18 R. Rajgopal vs State of T.N. on 7 October 1994,Supreme Court of India

Provided that the provisions contained in the first proviso to sub-section (1) of section 164 of the Code shall, so far it permits the presence of the advocate of the accused shall not apply in this case.

(2) The Magistrate shall provide to the child and his parents or his representative, a copy of the document specified under section 207 of the Code, upon the final report being filed by the police under section 173 of that Code.

Specimen order of recording statement of child rape victim

Before the Juvenile Justice Board,

Senapati District, Manipur

U/S 183 BNSS

JJB Misc Case no. 2 of 2024

Ref. FIR No 27(8)2024 WPS - SPT

U/S 64/331 BNS & 8 of POCSO Act 2012

The State of Manipur

Vs

Narayan Singh, 16 yrs

s/o Harideva Singh

Taranithoi Bazar,

PO & PS Senapati, Senapati District, Manipur

...CCL

ORDER

18/12/2024

This is an application filed by the CWPO WPS/SPT praying for recording the statement of the victim namely Baby Fajal, 11 yrs., d/o Md. Sadique of Taoroinai Bazaar, Senapati under

Section 183 BNSS in c/w FIR No 27(8)2024 WPS – SPT, U/S 64/331 BNS & 8 of POCSO Act 2012

Registered it as JJB Misc Case no. 2 of 2024

The CWPO is to produce the victim girl for recording her statement before the JMFC, Kangpokpi.

On completion of the said recording of statement of the victim girl, the SJPU WPS SPT is to intimate the Board.

Misc. case is disposed of accordingly.

(Signature)	**(Signature)**
Member	Member
Juvenile Justice Board	Juvenile Justice Board
Senapati District	Senapati District

PART 8

Bails

All cases of juveniles are bailable. Section 12(1) of JJ Act 2015 states that:

"When any person, who is apparently a child and is alleged to have committed a bailable or non-bailable offence, is apprehended or detained by the police or appears or brought before a Board, such person shall, notwithstanding anything contained in the Code of Criminal Procedure, 1973 or in any other law for the time being in force, be released on bail with or without surety or placed under the supervision of a probation officer or under the care of any fit person:

Provided that such person shall not be so released if there appears reasonable grounds for believing that the release is likely to bring that person into association with any known criminal or expose the said person to moral, physical or psychological danger or the person's release would defeat the ends of justice, and the Board shall record the reasons for denying the bail and circumstances that led to such a decision."

A specimen of order at the time of received of bail application

Date 17/10/2024

Application is filed by the mother of the CCL through the Ld. Counsel to release the CCL on Bail u/s 12 of JJ Act 2015.

Registered it as JJB Bail Case No. 3 of 2024.

Another copy of the application is also submitted for the Ld. APP, the same is forwarded to the Ld. APP.

Ld App is directed to call Bail Objection Report from the concerned PS.

Fixed 29/10/2024 for Bail hearing.

(Signature)	**(Signature)**
Member	Member
Juvenile Justice Board	Juvenile Justice Board
Senapati District	Senapati District

A sample of format of Call for Bail Objection Report by APP:

<u>IN LIEU OF MESSAGE FORM</u>

To
Officer-in-Charge
...............................P.S.

Date:...............

From APP to Principal Magistrate JJB, Senapati District

Memo No. JJB/SPT...

Please submit Bail Objection Report along with C/D before the Board, JJB/SPT for bail hearing on or before .... 2024 at 1:30 p.m. i/c with FIR No.................................., ... PS, u/s .... of CCL ...., s/o .... of .... without fail.

(Kh. Lakhi)
Asst. Public Prosecutor
Juvenile Justice Board,
Senapati District

There are some points to be remembered at the time of drafting a bail order. They are

    i.   Mention Bail Case No..

    ii.   Write the word "ORDER" just above the date.

    iii.   Mention Date of the Order underneath the word "Order".

    iv.   Names of the persons present, such as CCL, APP, Counsel for CCL, LPO, parents of the CCL, etc.

    v.   Mention prosecution history in brief.

    vi.   Mention perusal of Records.

    vii.   Record the Statement of LPO which is reflected in their SIR.

    viii.   Record the Statement of Counsel of the CCL and in the bail prayer application.

    ix.   Record the Statement of APP and Bail Objection Report.

    x.   Mention the Date of Birth of the CCL which is at the time of Commission of Offence.

    xi.   Write reasons for bail rejection or granting.

xii. If the bail is granted, give a directive to the Superintendent of Observation Home for the release of the CCL.

xiii. If the bail is granted, give some conditions under which the CCL should follow.

xiv. At the end of the order, write the word "Bail application is disposed of accordingly".

xv. At the base of the order give signatures of at least two persons among the Members and Principal Magistrate.

xvi. At the left space of the order sheet, take signatures of the present persons attending the hearing who are mentioned above.

In some petty or serious cases, the CCL may be granted bail at the time of first or second production (remand) before the Board. A sample model of order is given below:

Before the Juvenile Justice Board

Senapati District

JJB/SPT Bail Case No. 2 of 2024

Ref.: FIR No. 7(10)2024 SPT PS

u/s 21(c)/60(3) ND & PS Act

State

-Vs-

The State of Manipur

Vs

Narayan Singh, 16 yrs

s/o Harideva Singh

Yairipok,

PO & PS yairipok, Thoubal District, Manipur

... CCL

ORDER

11/11/2024

Present:

Mr. P P Singh, Ld Counsel for the CCL

Kh. Lakhi, Ld. Government Counsel for the State

SJPO of the case

Narayan Singh, CCL

Mrs. Ibemcha, mother of the CCL

The application is filed by Mrs Ibemcha mother of the CCL praying the board through Ld. Counsel to release the CCL on bail.

The allegation against the CCL is that on surprise check by a troop of 33 AR at Maram Bazar, on 10/10/2024 at 20:00 hrs. On Tata Truck bearing Regd. No. MNO1-12345 travelling from Imphal to Gauhati was halted. On the said Truck, one driver and 2(two) occupants namely (1) Narayan Singh & (2) Mr. ZZZ were travelling i.e., the above mentioned CCL. On checking the vehicle, 38 pouches of Brown Sugar weighing 10 grams each were recovered from the Truck which were hidden under seat cover. Approx. value of the seized brown sugar is Rs. 38,00,000/- (Rupees Thirty Eight Lakhs only). The driver of the Truck escaped from the spot taking advantage of the darkness. The seized Brown Sugar along with the other seized items & the 2 CCLs were handed over to Mao PS.

S. I. Simon, CWPO of the case submitted at his 2nd production prayer dated 20/10/2024 that the CCL was travelling in the same truck in which the suspected brown sugar was seized. However, the driver namely KKK of Yairipok, Thoubal District has fled from the spot. Efforts have been made to effect arrest of the driver. However, he is still absconding. It also came to light that the CCL is younger brother of the accused driver Mr. KKK who is still at large. On the same day, the I.O./ SJPU submitted before the Board that there is no evidence of involvement of the CCL in the offence charged leveled against the Tata truck driver. It could not be established the seized articles were related to the CCL.

The Counsel for the CCL submitted that the CCL is quite innocent to the police charge, no incriminating articles were recovered from the possession of the CCL to make out prima facie for charging against him. It is further submitted that the CCL is a student pursuing his further study in class –IX at U P C C School, Yairipok, Manipur after completion of class VIII. It is for his admission in Class IX. Thus, the petitioner further undertakes that she shall not make associate the CCL with any known criminals and she shall take care and look after all the steps of the CCL during his bail to prevent from becoming moral, physical and psychological danger. That, the Petitioner is ready and willing to accept any other conditions as may be imposed by the Hon'ble Board and she is ready to provide sufficient bond.

Ld App submits that the main accused were at large. The release of the CCL on bail shall affect to the investigation of the case. So, prayed the Board to keep further the CCL at the Observation Home.

Perused the materials on record and heard learned Govt. Counsel and Counsels for CCL. The CCL has been found to be aged about 16 yrs on the date of commission of the offence. Hence, he is a juvenile. Under section 12 of the JJ act 2015, it is provided that *"Such person shall not be released if there appears reasonable grounds for believing that the release is likely to bring him in association with any known criminal or expose him to moral, physical or psychological danger or the person's release will defeat the ends of justice".*

In the present case, no such factor has been brought on record to suggest the release of the CCL will *"bring him in association with any known criminal or expose him to moral, physical or psychological danger or the person's release will defeat the ends of justice".*

Bearing in mind, the observations based on the materials on records and submission of the Learned Counsels for both the state and the petitioner the Board is inclined to release the CCL on bail subject to furnishing PR bond of 50,000/- (Fifty Thousand Rupees) only along with one surety of the like amount, subject to the following conditions:

    a. That, the CCL shall not commit similar offence;

    b. That, the CCL shall refrain from any anti social activities;

    c. That, the CCL shall not hamper investigation;

    d. That, the CCL shall not tamper with evidence;

    e. That, the CCL shall appear before the board as and when directed;

    f. The CCL should submit a surety bond of Rs. 50000/- (Fifty Thousand) only.

The Bail prayer is allowed. The objection report stands rejected.

Announced in the presence of the board members and counsels for the petitioner and state including the CCL.

The matter is hereby disposed of.

(Signature)　　　　**(Signature)**
Member　　　　Member
Juvenile Justice Board　　　　Juvenile Justice Board
Senapati District　　　　Senapati District

Bail Bond and Surety are checked and verified and found correct. The CCL is directed to appear before the Board on 120/11/2024.

(Signature)　　　　**(Signature)**
Member　　　　Member
Juvenile Justice Board　　　　Juvenile Justice Board
Senapati District　　　　Senapati District

A model of Regular Bail Order

Before the Juvenile Justice Board
Senapati District
JJB/SPT Bail Case No. 14 of 2024

Ref. FIR No. 11(11)2024 SPT PS
u/s 303(2)/317(2)/3(5) BNS

The State of Manipur
Vs
Narayan Singh, 16 yrs
s/o Harideva Singh
Taranithoi Bazar,

PO & PS Senapati, Senapati District, Manipur

...CCL

ORDER

23/12/2024

Present:

Mr. P P Singh, Ld Counsel for the CCL

Kh. Lakhi, Ld. Government Counsel for the State

Narayan Singh CCL

Taoroinai Luwang, Ld. LPO

Mrs. Ibemcha, mother of the CCL

Ld Counsel for the CCL submitted the application praying the Board to release the CCL on bail u/s 12 of JJ Act 2015.

In the present case, the CCL was first brought before the board on 19 November, 2024 i/c with the above mentioned FIR.

Brief facts leading to the present case is that on 18/11/2024 at 02:00 pm the complainant received a reliable information that the accused person namely Md Amrish Khan of Taranithoi Bazar who indulged in vehicle lifting is staying at the accused house with one stolen two-wheeler. Acting on the information, the complainant informed to the senior officers and under their supervision, the complainant with his team immediately rushed to the said accused house and conducted search. In that the accused person Md Amrish Khan (18) s/o Md Naoba of Taranithoi Bazar was found at his house and detained for verification.

The allegation is that on further interrogation, the accused disclosed the name of the Juvenile, i.e., Narayan Singh, 16 years, s/o Haridava Singh of Taranithoi Bazar, PO Senapati, Senapati PS, who was also involved in the theft.

SI P. Simon, CWPO/IO of the case submitted his Bail Objection Report of the case on today. In the report, the CCL was involved u/s 379/411/34 IPC in the said incident. The CCL was involved in selling the stolen two-wheeler by knowing that it was a stolen property. The CCL got their due share. The CCL concealed the fact by simply lying and giving false statements. So, the board is prayed to reject the bail move.

The IO of the case further submitted that there is some contradiction on the statements of the CCL and the accused. The CCL is required to be interviewed when necessary.

Ld. APP submitted that CCL Narayan was involved in the act of theft. He has knowledge of the act of theft. He has knowledge of the offence. The CCL has got its due share from the sale of the vehicle.

The petitioner states that the CCL is quite innocent of the offence alleged against him and that no incriminating article was found from his possession at the time of his apprehension.

Further, the CCL is pursuing Class XI Science at Taranithoi Bazar at which Council of Higher Secondary Education, Manipur Class-XI Examination 2024 is going on from 20 February 2024 till 29 March 2024

Perused the record and heard learned govt. Counsel and Counsel for CCL. The CCL has been found to be above 16 yrs on the date commission of the offence. Hence, he is a juvenile. Under section 12 of the JJ act 2015, it is provided that in case any CCL is apprehended in connection with any offence, he has to be released on bail unless such release *"is likely to bring him in association with any known criminal or expose him to moral, physical or psychological danger or the person's release will defeat the ends of justice".*

In the present case, no such factor has been brought on record to suggest the release of the CCL will bring him *"bring him in association with any known criminal or expose him to moral, physical or psychological danger or the person's release will defeat the ends of justice".*

It is also not stated that the release of the CCL will lead to hampering in investigation or tamper with evidence. In the circumstances, further detention of the CCL will be prejudicial to his interest, hence the CCL is granted bail on his furnishing Bail Bond of Rs. 20000 and surety of like amount and on the condition that the CCL will appear before the board as when directed by this Board and that he shall not hamper the investigation or tamper with evidence.

The CCLs should corporate the IO of the case when necessary.

Bail petition is accordingly disposed of.

(signature)	**(signature)**
Member	Member
Juvenile Justice Board	Juvenile Justice Board
Senapati District	Senapati District

Guardian Bond is furnished as directed. Checked, verified and accepted. The CCL is directed to appear on 03/01/2025.

(signature)   **(signature)**

Member   Member

Juvenile Justice Board   Juvenile Justice Board

Senapati District   Senapati District

Specimen of Interim Bail Order

Before the Juvenile Justice Board

Senapati District

JJB/SPT Bail Case No. 27 of 2024

Ref: FIR No. 27(11)2024 SPT PS

u/s 64 BNS and 8 of POCSO Act 2012

The State of Manipur

Vs

Narayan Singh, 16 yrs

s/o Harideva Singh

Taranithoi Bazar,

PO & PS Senapati, Senapati District, Manipur

<u>ORDER</u>

5/12/2024

Present:

Mr. P P Singh, Ld Counsel for the CCL

Kh. Lakhi, Ld. Government Counsel for the State

Narayan Singh, CCL

Taoroinai Luwang, Ld. LPO

Mrs. Ibemcha, mother of the CCL

This is an application filed by the mother of the CCL praying to release the CCL on bail under section 12 of JJ Act 2015 along with an interim bail on account of appearing the final examination of the CCL.

Registered it as JJB Bail Case No. 27 of 2024.

Ld APP for state and Ld Counsel for the CCL are also present before the board.

It is submitted that the final examination of the said CCL would be starting from 10th December 2024 and conclude on 20th December 2024. The Ld Counsel also appended annexure A/2 which is the routine / time table for the said examination.

The issue was pondered upon by the board with the best interest of the CCL in mind. The mother was heard at length and it was submitted that the CCL's residence had been changed to another place and there was no immediate possibility of the CCL and the alleged victim coming into contact physically with each other.

Considering the best interest of the child and the commitment of the mother/ guardian that she would personally ensure that such offence would not be continuing again, the board is of the considered view that prayer for interim bail be allowed on the following conditions;

1.   That, the CCL shall be allowed to leave the observation home w.e.f. 05th December 2024.
2.   That, the CCL shall report back to the observation home on 21st December 2024 on or before 2 pm.
3.   That, the CCL shall not commit similar act.

4. That, in the event of any adverse finding or report, at any time that the board may deem necessary, the interim bail shall stand terminated.
5. That, the CCL shall be allowed to leave the observation home only subject to the Guardian bond being furnished amounting to fifty Thousand Rupees.

Considering the facts and circumstances, the Board is of the considered view to allow the prayer for interim bail on the conditions as mentioned above and the regular bail shall be heard and pondered on filing the objection report from the prosecution.

Fixed 21/12/2024 for report to the Superintendent of Observation Home.

<table>
<tr><td>(Signature)</td><td>(Signature)</td></tr>
<tr><td>Member</td><td>Member</td></tr>
<tr><td>Juvenile Justice Board</td><td>Juvenile Justice Board</td></tr>
<tr><td>Senapati District</td><td>Senapati District</td></tr>
</table>

Statutory Bail (Default Bail)

Statutory bail also known as default bail is a legal right for the CCL to be release on if the SJPU has failed to submit final investigation Report (Charge-Sheet) within a specified period u/s 187(3) BNSS.

The proviso of sub-section (2) of section 167 (CrPC) is a beneficial provision for curing the mischief of indefinitely prolonging the investigation on the expiry of the said period of 90 days or 60 days, as the case may be, an indefeasible right accrues in favour of the accused for being released on bail on account of default by the investigating agency in the completion of the investigation within the period prescribed. The accused is entitled to be releases on bail, if he is prepared to and does furnish the bail as directed by the Magistrate; *Uday Mohanlal Acharya v. State of Maharastra, AIR 2001 SC 1910: 2001 AIR SCW 1500: (2001) 5 SCC 453: 2001 Cr LJ 1832 (SC).*[19]

Specimen order

Before the Juvenile Justice Board
Senapati District
JJB/SPT Bail Case No. 3 of 2025

Ref.:- FIR No. 35(8)2024 SPT PS
U/S 17/20 UA (P) A. Act.

The State of Manipur
Vs
Narayan Singh, 16 yrs
s/o Harideva Singh
Taranithoi Bazar,
PO & PS Cachar, Cachar District, Assam
...CCL
<u>ORDER</u>
14/03/2025

Board sitting is held today. The CCL namely Narayan Singh, 16 yrs, s/o Harideva Singh of Taranithoi Bazar, PO & PS Cachar, Cachar District, Assam is produced before the Board.

---

19 Uday Mohanlal Acharya v. State of Maharastra, AIR 2001 SC 1910: 2001 AIR SCW 1500: (2001) 5 SCC 453: 2001 Cr LJ 1832 (SC)

The elder brother of the CCL and guardian of the CCL are also present.

Legal Aid Counsel /Panel Layer Mr. P P Singh is also present.

Record shows that statutory period is lapsed for keeping the CCL at the observation Home. But no FR is submitted till date.

Hence, the CCL is released on bail on executing Guardian Bond of Rs. 20,000/- and as per rules since the CCL is from Cachar District, Assam, the Guardian Bond is to be furnished by a Guardian/Relative of the CCL preferably from Senapati District.

(Signature)   **(Signature)**
Member   Member
Juvenile Justice Board   Juvenile Justice Board
Senapati District   Senapati District

PART 9

Preliminary Assessment

Preliminary Assessment means the assessment whether the CCL has (a) the **physical** and **mental capacity** to commit the offence, (b) whether he/she understands the **consequences** of the offence and (c) **Circumstances** in which they allegedly committed the offence under section 15, JJ Act 2015.

When an offence is committed by a CCL who is above sixteen years of age and the offence committed is found to be heinous in nature, the Board shall conduct a preliminary assessment with regard to his mental and physical capacity to commit such offence, ability to understand the consequences of the offence and circumstances in which he allegedly committed the offence and may pass order in accordance with the provisions of sub-section (3) of section 18 of JJ Act.

Where the Board after preliminary assessment may pass an order that the CCL is in need for a trial as an adult, the case should be transferred to the Children's Court having jurisdiction for trial of such cases u/s 18 o(3) of JJ Act.

Physical capacity is simply understood the physical strength of the CCL to commit the offence.

Further, **Mental capacity** means:

a. To identify children with psychiatric, mental health issues and/or personality issues,
b. Experiences of abuse and trauma,
c. Substance abuse problems,
d. Intellectual disability,
e. Mental health disorder/ developmental disability,
f. Treatment/ interventions provided so far, etc.

> *Source: **Guidance Notes on Preliminary Assessment Report for Children in Conflict with Law, Community Child & Adolescent Mental Health Service Project, Dept. of Child & Adolescent Psychiatry, National Institute of Mental Health and Neuro Sciences (NIMHANS), Bengaluru***

Circumstances of the commission of offence can be identified by studying the following areas.

a. Family history and relationships (child's living arrangements, parental relationships, child's emotional relationship & attachment to parents, illness & alcoholism in the family, domestic violence and marital discord if any).
b. School and education (child's school attendance, Last grade attended, reasons for child not attending school- whether it is due to financial issues or lack of motivation, school refusal, corporal punishment).
c. Work experience/ Child labour (why the child had to work/ how child found the place of work, where he was working / hours of work and amount of remuneration received, was there any physical/

emotional abuse by the employer and also regarding negative influence the child may have encountered in the workplace regarding substance abuse etc.).

d. Peer relationships (adverse peer influence in the context of substance use/ rule-breaking/ inappropriate sexual behaviour/school attendance)

e. Experiences of trauma and abuse (physical, sexual & emotional Abuse experiences)

*Source; **Guidance Notes on Preliminary Assessment Report for Children in Conflict with Law, Community Child & Adolescent Mental Health Service Project, Dept. of Child & Adolescent Psychiatry, National Institute of Mental Health and Neuro Sciences (NIMHANS), Bengaluru***

Understanding Consequences of the offence:

Consequences may be divided into two (i) immediate consequence and (ii) far sighted consequence. Immediate consequence shall be known by all juveniles. By the act of their action the victim shall be died is obviously known. Our concern is to whether the CCL understand the far-sighted consequence.

The language used in section 15 is "the ability to understand the consequences of the offence". The expression used is in plurality i.e., "consequences" of the offence and, therefore, would not just be confined to the immediate consequence of the offence or that the occurrence of the offence would only have its consequence upon the victim but it would also take within its ambit the consequences which may fall upon not only the victim as a result of the assault, but also on the family of the victim, on the child, his family, and that too not only immediate consequences but also the far-reaching consequences in future. Consequences could be in material/physical form but also affecting the mind and the psychology of the child for all times to come. The consequences of the offence could be numerous and manifold which cannot be just linked to a framework; and, for this purpose, the overall picture as also future consequences with reference to the facts of the case are required to be consciously analysed by the Board; *AB (2 juveniles) V State of Chhatisgarh, 2022. CPR No. 625 Of 2022, High Court of Chhatisgarh.*[20]

The Board may take the assistance of experienced psychologists or psycho-social workers or other experts. As a first step to conduct preliminary assessment (a) Calculate the age of the child whether he is above sixteen and below eighteen years of age; and (b) Check whether the offence is heinous in nature. If so, the Board shall pass an Order, like the following.

A model order referring the CCL to experts for examining mental status

<u>ORDER</u>

21/08/2024

The CCL is produced before the Board.

Ld. Counsel for the CCL and the State are present. Ld. LPO is present.

Perused the records on material.

---

20 AB (2 juveniles) V State of Chhatisgarh, 2022. CPR No. 625 Of 2022, High Court of Chhatisgarh

The CCL is found his Date of Birth as 15/8/2008. He was 16 years 11 months and 6 days at the time of the commission of offence. The offence he has committed is heinous in nature.

The board shall conduct a preliminary assessment with regard to his mental and physical capacity to commit the offence and test the ability to understand the consequences of offence.

The Board has observed the mental attitude of the CCL. To conduct the mental assessment of the CCL is paramount important as he had committed a heinous offence i.e., murder.

The Superintendent of Observation Home is directed to produce the CCL in the Department of Clinical Psychology, Regional Institute of Medical Sciences, Imphal for conducting mental assessment, and further to produce before a psychiatrist whether the CCL has psychiatric disorders.

Send a copy of this order to the Department of Clinical Psychology, Regional Institute of Medical Sciences and the Superintendent of Observation Home.

(Signature)	(Signature)
Member	Member
Juvenile Justice Board	Juvenile Justice Board
Senapati District	Senapati District

A model letter for testing Mental Status

Office of the Juvenile Justice Board,
Senapati District.

Memo No. JJB/SPT/2024/12   Date. 21/09/2024

To

The Head
Department of Clinical Psychology
Regional Institute of medical Sciences,
Imphal.
Subject: To conduct Mental Assessment of CCL.

Madam,

With reference to the above mentioned subject, we would like to bring to your kind notice that as per provision of section 15 of Juvenile Justice (Care and Protection of Children) Act, 2015, in case of a juvenile who is above 16 years of age and below the age of 18 years is alleged to have committed a heinous offence, preliminary assessment has to be conducted to ascertain the mental capacity of the juvenile to commit the offence at the time of commission of the offence. For conducting such preliminary assessment, the psychological test is required in order to enable the Board to correctly assess the mental capacity of the juvenile.

Such preliminary assessment is required to be conducted in one case pending before the board i/c with FIR No. 55(10)2024 WPS/SPT, u/s 103(1) BNS. The prosecution history of the case is that on 23/10/2024 the CCL Narayan Singh, 16 yrs, s/o Harideva Singh of Taranithoi Bazar, PO & PS Senapati, Senapati District murdered an old man with a dagger.

In this regard, you are directed to conduct his mental status and capacity to commit the alleged offence and understand the consequences of it.

Thanking you,

(signature)   (signature)

Member   Member

Juvenile Justice Board   Juvenile Justice Board

Senapati District   Senapati District

A specimen order of transferring to Children's Court

BEFORE THE JUVENILE JUSTICE BOARD, SENAPATI DISTRICT

<u>FIR No. 15(7) 2024 WPS/ SPT</u>

u/s 64 BNS, 6 POCSO Act

The State of Manipur

Vs

Narayan Singh, 16 yrs

s/o Harideva Singh

Taranithoi Bazar,

PO & PS Senapati, Senapati District, Manipur

CCL

<u>ORDER</u>

15th October, 2024

<u>**Present:**</u>

Mr. P P Singh, Ld Counsel for the CCL

Kh. Lakhi, Ld. Government Counsel for the State

Narayan Singh, CCL

Taoroinai Luwang, Ld. LPO

Mrs. Ibemcha, mother of the CCL

The CCL is present along with the counsel and guardian. The case is fixed for finding on preliminary assessment of the CCL namely Narayan Singh, aged 16 yrs, s/o Harideva Singh, Taranithoi Bazar, PO & PS Senapati, Senapati District, Manipur.

On being referred by this Board, the above mentioned CCL was examined by Dr. N. Ashalata Devi, Asst. Professor and Ranibala Takhellamabm of Department of Clinical Psychology, RIMS Imphal. Their findings on the CCL are briefly stated as follows:-

From the clinical observation and test findings, it can be concluded that the CCL has no cognitive impairment, no features of anxiety and depression however he has Moderate PTSD Symptoms"

The CCL was also examined by this board, brief summary/ opinion of this board on the basis of their examination is stated as below:-

CCL has passed class –X examination, is found to be ambitious and career oriented, wants to appear NDA examination. The CCL expressed regrets and anger of the incident.

Also perused the report filed by the Counsellor, Smt. P. Anjali Devi, Counsellor of Observation Home. The report narrates the CCLs' account of the incident, at the end note it is mentioned that in her opinion the CCL was not aware of the consequence. On examination of the counsellor, she stated that she gave her opinion on the basis of their denial that they committed offence of murder.

Perused the SIR submitted by Ld. LPO.

Perused the materials on record including Psychological Test Report, Counseling report, SIR, SBR and the Final Investigation Report. After due consideration of the relevant record, this board is of the opinion that the above mentioned CCL has the ability and sufficient maturity to understand the nature of the case and also that such acts are morally and legally wrong, He is also well capable of understanding the consequence of such act.

On the basis of the Psychological and medical report and as well as examination by this board, we are also of the opinion that the CCL has the Physical and Mental Capacity to commit such offence and understand the consequences of the offence.

For the reasons discussed above, this board is of the opinion that there is a need for trial of the CCL as an adult as per the provisions of Juvenile Justice (Care and Protection of Children) Act.2015. Hence, the case of the CCL namely Narayan Singh, aged 16 yrs is forwarded to the Hon'ble Children Court, Senapati District.

The SJPU of WPS/SPT is directed to take necessary steps for production of the CCL before the Hon'ble Children Court, Senapati District. And transfered the CCL from the present Observation Home to Place of Safety.

(Signature)	**(Signature)**	**(Signature)**
Member	Principal Magistrate	Member
Juvenile Justice Board	Juvenile Justice Board	Juvenile Justice Board
Senapati District	Senapati District	Senapati District

Copies may be sent to the following:

1. the Hon'ble Children Court, Senapati District;
2. I.O. of the Case;
3. Superintendent of Observation Home; and
4. Superintendent of Place of Safety.

PART 10

Extension of Period for Enquiry

The inquiry of a case must be completed within a period of six months from the date of first production before the Board. In the petty cases, the inquiry must be completed within four months from the date of first production of the CCL before the board. Otherwise, acceptance should be sought from the concerned Chief Judicial Magistrate. Thus,

a. Inquiry (trial) shall be completed within a period of four months from first production of CCL.[21]

b. If it is not completed within this period, a two months time may be extended. The reason of such extension may be recorded in writing.[22]

c. Even after the extension of time, the proceeding of petty offence remains inconclusive, the case shall be terminated.[23]

d. For further extension of time in the cases of Serious and Heinous offences, the same shall be granted by the Chief Judicial Magistrate or Chief Metropolitan

---

21 Under section 14(2) JJ Act 2015
22 Under section 14(2) JJ Act 2015
23 Under section 14(4) JJ Act 2015

Magistrate. The reason of such extension may be recorded in writing.[24]

e. As per dictum of the JJ Act, inquiry should be initiated from the first production of CCL before the Board. On the other hand, the Board is helpless unless the Final Investigation Report (Charge -Sheet) is submitted by the investigating police officer.

A Specimen Letter is given below for seeking of extension of period from Chief Judicial Magistrate

The Juvenile Justice Board,
Senapati District, Manipur

Memo No JJB/SPT/2025/01   Date 2 January 2025

Ref. FIR No. 60(7)2024 SPT-PS.
U/S 101 BNSS

The State of Manipur
Vs
Narayan Singh, 16 yrs
s/o Harideva Singh
Taranithoi Bazar,
PO & PS Senapati, Senapati District, Manipur
...CCL

To,
The Chief Judicial Magistrate,
Senapati District
Subject: Prayer for extension of period for enquiry.

Hon'ble Madam,

---

24 Under section 14(4) JJ Act 2015

With due respect, we the undersigned, on behalf of JJB/ SPT, would like to state the following few lines for your kind perusal and necessary action.

That JJB/SPT Case No. 3 of 2024 i/w. FIR No. 60(7)2024 SPT-PS. U/S 101 BNSS of CCL Narayan Singh, 16 yrs, s/o Harideva Singh of Taranithoi Bazar, PO & PS Senapati, Senapati District, Manipur is in the stage of inquiry since 12 July 2024. However, the inquiry could not be completed in the stipulated time due to non-appearance of the CCL. So, you are requested kindly to extend further two months period to complete the inquiry of the case and justice be delivered.

Yours faithfully

<table>
<tr><td>(Signature)</td><td>(Signature)</td></tr>
<tr><td>Member</td><td>Member</td></tr>
<tr><td>Juvenile Justice Board</td><td>Juvenile Justice Board</td></tr>
<tr><td>Senapati District</td><td>Senapati District</td></tr>
</table>

Further, a sample of specimen letter is given below for seeking further extension of period inquiry

Office of the Juvenile Justice Board,
Senapati District, Manipur

Memo No JJB/SPT/2025/5   Date 24 March 2025

Ref. FIR3 No. 60(7)2024 SPT-PS.
U/S 101 BNSS

The State of Manipur
Vs
Narayan Singh, 16 yrs

s/o Harideva Singh
Taranithoi Bazar,
PO & PS Senapati, Senapati District, Manipur

To,
The Chief Judicial Magistrate,
Imphal East District,
Lamphel Pat, Imphal
Subject: Prayer for extension of period for enquiry.

Hon'ble Madam,

With due respect, we the undersigned, on behalf of JJB/ SPT, would like to state the following few lines for your kind perusal and necessary action.

That JJB/SPT Inquiry Case No. 1 of 2024 FIR No. 74(9)2024 SPT PS, U/S 363 IPC of the CCL Narayan Singh, 16 yrs, s/o Harideva Singh of Taranithoi Bazar, PO & PS Senapati, Senapati District, Manipur in the stage of inquiry.

As per Memo. No. CJM/SPT/2024/521-22 dated 25th May 2024 i/c with the above mentioned case, the Ld CJM, Senapati directed to this Board that *"no further extension of time shall be granted after this. The Board Members must endeavor to dispose the case within 2 months from today."* beyond 25 July 2024.

However, the inquiry could not be completed within the stipulated time ordered by the Chief Judicial Magistrate, Senapati District due to non-appearance of witnesses, one day postponement due to the condolence of demise of an advocate by AMBA, and flood havoc in the State.

So, you are requested kindly to extend further two months period to complete the inquiry of the case and justice be delivered.

Yours faithfully

(Signature)   **(Signature)**
Member   Member
Juvenile Justice Board Senapati   Juvenile Justice Board
District   Senapati District

Education

Education shall be provided to all juveniles according to age and ability during the stay at the child care institution including Observation Homes. There shall be a range of educational opportunities including mainstream inclusive schools, bridge school, open schooling, non-formal education and learning and input from special educators where needed. Whenever necessary, extra coaching shall be made to school going juveniles. Section 53 JJ Act 2015 mentions of the right to education and its fundamental act: Right to Free and Compulsory Education Act, 2009.[25]

Rule No. 36 of JJ Rules 2016 provides the range of educational opportunities to be facilitated to the children including juvenile. It includes main stream education, extra coaching, other educational support programmes. Specimen of School admission, order of appearing examination and seeking special educator from the government is given here.

---

25 P88, Rights of Juveniles by Athokpam Chinglemba Luwang, 2019

Specimen order of School Admission

Before the Juvenile Justice Board,
Senapati District, Manipur
JJB Misc Case No. 27 of 2024

FIR No. 15(8) 2024 WPS/ SPT

u/s 64 BNS

The State of Manipur

Vs

Narayan Singh, 16 yrs

s/o Harideva Singh

Taranithoi Bazar,

PO & PS Senapati, Senapati District, Manipur

...CCL

ORDER

4/12/2024

Present:

Mr. P P Singh, Ld Counsel for the CCL

Kh. Lakhi, Ld. Government Counsel for the State

Narayan Singh CCL

Taoroinai Luwang, Ld. LPO

Mr P R Singh, Superintendent of the Observation Home

1. The Present petition is filed by Ld Counsel for the CCL for allowing the CCL to take admission in class XI, Arts.
2. The Ld. Counsel of the CCL submitted that the CCL is presently staying at Observation Home, Takyelpat and he has passed class X examination conducted by

Board of Secondary Education Manipur (BOSEM) in the year 2024. Since the CCL had cleared aforesaid examination, the CCL wish to take admission and attend school at Model Higher Secondary School which is very near to Juvenile Observation Home, Takyelpat, Imphal West District.

3. The Ld. Counsel further submitted that if the CCL is not allowed to admit and attend school at Model Higher Secondary School, the academic career of the CCL shall be badly affected and it cannot be compensated in monetary terms.

4. Kh. Lakhi, Ld APP submitted the board to decide what is the best for the interest of the child.

5. Superintendent of the Observation Home submitted that in the best interest of the child, the Board is prayed to allow his admission in the school and attend the school.

6. Section 36 (1) of JJ Rules 2016 clearly states that *"Every institution shall provide education to all children according to the age and ability, both inside the institution or outside, as per requirement.*

    (2) There shall be a range of educational opportunities including, mainstream inclusive schools, bridge school, open schooling, non-formal education and learning where needed."

7. Considering all the antecedents and circumstances, the prayer is allowed.

8. Superintendent of the Observation Home is directed to take necessary steps.

9. Send a copy of this order to Superintendent of the Observation Home.

10. Application is disposed of accordingly.

(signature)   **(signature)**
Member   Member
Juvenile Justice Board   Juvenile Justice Board
Senapati District   Senapati District

Order to attend private tuition class

Before the Juvenile Justice Board,
Senapati District, Manipur
<u>JJB Misc Case No. 27 of 2024</u>

FIR No. 15(4) 2024 WPS/ SPT

u/s 363 IPC,

The State of Manipur

Vs

Narayan Singh, 16 yrs
s/o Harideva Singh
Taranithoi Bazar,
PO & PS Senapati, Senapati District, Manipur
...CCL
<u>ORDER</u>
13/11/2024

<u>**Present:**</u>

Mr. P P Singh, Ld Counsel for the CCL

Kh. Lakhi, Ld. Government Counsel for the State

Narayan Singh, CCL

Taoroinai Luwang, Ld. LPO

Harideva Singh, father of CCL

1. The Present petition is filed by Harideva Singh, father of CCL on behalf of his son Narayan Singh for allowing his son to attend private tuition class.

2. Brief facts leading to the present case is that the CCL is presently staying at Observation Home, Takyelpat and now pursuing B.Sc. 1st Semester at NG Mani College, Khurai, Chairenthong, IE.

3. The Ld. Counsel of the CCL submitted that the private tuition centre is at Kwakeithel Thiyam Leikai, Imphal West. The duration of the tuition shall be ranged for around eight months beginning by 2nd December 2024. Board is prayed to allow him to attend the said private tuition class.

4. Harideva Singh, father of the CCL submitted that all the responsibilities of caring and escorting of the CCL shall be borne by him.

5. Section 36 (1) of JJ Rules 2016 clearly states that *"Every institution shall provide education to all children according to the age and ability, both inside the institution or outside, as per requirement.*

   (2) There shall be a range of educational opportunities including, mainstream inclusive schools, bridge school, open schooling, non-formal education and learning where needed."

6. Considering all the antecedents, the prayer is allowed on the following conditions:

7. The CCL shall be taken out from the Observation Home from 4:30 a.m. onwards and shall be brought back home before 8 a.m. of every working day starting from 2nd December 2024 to 2nd July 2025.

8. All the responsibilities of caring and escorting of the CCL should be borne by the Father of the CCL.

9. Send a copy of this order to Superintendent of the Observation Home

10. Misc Case is disposed of accordingly.

(signature)   (signature)

Member   Member

Juvenile Justice Board Juvenile Justice Board

Senapati District   Senapati District

Specimen Order of Instruction to Superintendent to provide Education or Vocational Training

Before the Juvenile Justice Board,

Senapati District, Manipur

<u>JJB Misc Case No. 27 of 2024</u>

FIR No. 15(4) 2024 SPT

u/s 363 IPC,

The State of Manipur

Vs

Lukram Dhanaraj, 15 yrs

s/o Harideva Singh

Taranithoi Bazar,

PO & PS Senapati, Senapati District, Manipur

...CCL

<u>Order</u>

24/07/2024

Present CCL namely Lukram Dhanaraj, mother of the CCL and APP for the state.

Mother of the CCL has submitted that she wants the CCL to keep at Observation Home for some time. She has apprehension that the CCL would commit such similar offence if he is released. So, she prayed the Board to provide education for the CCL.

CCL submitted he studied up to class IV only, and he has poor understanding of education.

The prayer is accepted by considering the best interest of the child.

The Superintendent of Observation Home is to do the necessary steps for providing the CCL informal education and vocational training.

Produce the CCL on 1/8/2024.

(signature)   (signature)
Member   Member
Juvenile Justice Board   Juvenile Justice Board
Senapati District   Senapati District

Copy to:

The Superintendent of Observation Home.

Provision of Special Educator

There was on order that facilitated a juvenile by providing special educator incorporating with Department of Education Government of Manipur. I reproduce herewith the same order passed by the board for kind reference with concealment of the identity of the CCL. And the same can be considered historical. To the reply of this order, the department of Education,

Government of Manipur provided a special educator to provide education to the CCL. This step was the first of its kind incorporating with the Department of Education in the history of Juvenile Justice System in Manipur.

Before the Juvenile Justice Board,
Senapati District, Manipur
JJB/SNPT Misc case No. 1 of 2022

Reference: 11(3)21 KPI P.S.

U/s 326/302 IPC

The State of Manipur

Vs

Narayan Singh, 16 yrs
s/o Harideva Singh
Taranithoi Bazar,
PO & PS Senapati, Senapati District, Manipur
...Child in Conflict with Law (CCL)

ORDER

15th June 2022

The Application is filed by Mr Niraj Tamang, cousin brother of the CCL praying the Board to provide education to the CCL.

The CCL is presently staying at the Observation Home for Boys, Takyelpat, Imphal. Today, he has completed one year, one month and 5 days.

As per record, he was born on 17/09/2006.He has completed 15 years 8 months and 29 days.

As per record, he had attended School up to class V at the Sanju (not real name) Junior High School, Charoi Khullen (not real name the school), Senapati District. He has been out of school since then for the last 6 years. He has now become a child of Special Needs. So, he is required to be taught and guided by *Special Educators* under *Samagra Shiksha.*

The same is also mandated in the article 3 of The National Education Policy 2020 under the title of **Curtailing Dropout Rates and Ensuring Universal Access to Education at All Levels.** Thus,

"... 3.2. There are two overall initiatives that will be undertaken to bring children who have dropped out back to school and to prevent further children from dropping out. The first is to provide effective and sufficient infrastructure so that all students have access to safe and engaging school education at all levels from pre-primary school to Grade 12."

Further, sub-section 2 of section 36 of Juvenile Justice (Care and Protection of Children) Rules, 2016 states that *"There shall be a range of educational opportunities including, mainstream inclusive schools, bridge school, open schooling, non formal education and learning where needed."*

Bearing in mind the Principle of the Best Interest of the Child, the CCL should get benefit of education and help him to develop his inner potential.

Considering all circumstances and provisions, the **Director of Education (Schools), Government of Manipur is directed to avail *Special Educators* under *Samagra Shiksha* to the CCL.** Send a copy of this order to the Director of Education (Schools), Government of Manipur for information and to do the needful at the earliest. Also, send copies of this order to the Director, Social Welfare, Government of Manipur and Superintendent of Observation Home for Boys, Takyelpat.

G. Tarunkumar Sharma, DeO to take step.

Fixed 24/06/2022 for compliance of this Order.

Signed/-	*Signed/-*	*Signed/-*
Member	i/c Principal	Member
Juvenile Justice	Magistrate	Juvenile Justice
Board	Juvenile Justice Board	Board
Senapati	Senapati District	Senapati District
District		

PART 12

Transferring to Child Welfare Committee

A child who is alleged to have committed an offence may be found to be a child in need of care and protection (CNCP). Whether a CCL is being a CNCP or not can be understood only after examination of Social Background Report (SBR) and Social Investigation Report (SIR). Once the CCL is found to be a CNCP, the board should recommend the CCL to the concerned CWC for his CNCP status.

Under section 8 (g) JJ Act 2015, it is mentioned that:

"transferring to the Committee, matters concerning the child alleged to be in conflict with law, stated to be in need of care and protection at any stage, thereby recognising that a child in conflict with law can also be a child in need of care simultaneously and there is a need for the Committee and the Board to be both involved;"

Some tips for recommendation

i. Record in written in the order the vulnerable conditions of the CCL which mentioned in the SIR and SBR. For example, the CCL has no parents or guardians to be looked after. He is only 14 years old. He was a child labourer.

ii. JJB may recommend the CCL directly the concerned CWC or may give directive the concerned District Child Protection Unit (DCPU) to take step. If the CCL is outside of the State, recommendation directly to the concerned Social Welfare Department or Child Welfare Directorate would be appropriate.

Specimen order

<u>ORDER</u>

14/03/2025

Board sitting is held today. The CCL namely Narayan Singh, 14 yrs, s/o Harideva Singh of Wangkhei, Imphal East District is produced before the Board.

Legal Aid Counsel /Panel Layer Mr. P P Singh is present.

Ld APP is present.

Perused the materials on record. Studied SBR and SIR.

Records show that the CCL has no parents or guardians to be looked after. He is only 14 years old. He is a child labourer

Section 2. (14)(vi) of JJ Act 2015 mentions that:

"who does not have parents and no one is willing to take care of, or whose parents have abandoned or surrendered him."

Thus, the CCL is found to be a CNCP.

Hence, this board is recommending the CCL to CWC, Imphal East District to consider his CNCP status.

DCPU, Imphal East District is directed to put up the matter before the CWC, Imphal East District.

Fixed 25/3/2025 for further proceeding.

(Signature)   **(Signature)**

Member   Member

Juvenile Justice Board   Juvenile Justice Board

Senapati District   Senapati District

Letter to DCPU for necessary action

Before the Juvenile Justice Board

Senapati District

Memo No. JJB/SPT/2025/07   Date 14/3/2025

Ref.:- FIR No. 35(12)2024 SPT PS
U/S 317(2) BNS

The State of Manipur

Vs

Narayan Singh, 16 yrs

s/o Harideva Singh

Wangkhei, Imphal East District

...CCL

To,
District Child Protection Officer
Imphal East district

Sir,

I have the honour to state that I am forwarding the extract copy of the "Order" passed by Juvenile Justice Board, Senapati District on 14 March, 2025 i/c with the above mentioned FIR and CCL for your compliance.

Thanking you,

Enclosed: Extract copy of Order.

Yours Sincerely
(Signature)
Data Entry Operator
The Juvenile Justice Board
Senapati District

PART 13

Leave of Absence from Child Care Institution

During the stay at the Child Care Institution, the CCL may take leave of absence from the institution upto seven days under section 98(1) of Juvenile Justice (Care and Protection of Children) Act, 2015. It mentions that:

"The Committee or the Board, as the case may be, may permit leave of absence to any child, to allow him, on special occasions like examination, marriage of relatives, death of kith or kin or accident or serious illness of parent or any emergency of like nature, under supervision, for a period generally not exceeding seven days in one instance, excluding the time taken in journey."

A Model Order of Leave of Absence

Before the Juvenile Justice Board,
Senapati District, Manipur
<u>JJB/SPT Misc Case No. 14 of 2024</u>
Ref: FIR No. 19(10) 2024 WPS/ SPT, u/s 6 POCSO Act

The State of Manipur
Vs
Narayan Singh, 16 yrs
s/o Harideva Singh

Taranithoi Bazar,

PO & PS Senapati, Senapati District, Manipur

...Child in Conflict with Law (CCL)

Present:

Mr. P P Singh, Ld Counsel for the CCL

Narayan Singh, CCL

Harideva Singh, the father of the CCL

<u>ORDER</u>

8/11/2024

1. Application is filed by Harideva Singh, the father of the CCL for allowing him to participate in the Shradha (death) ceremony of the maternal uncle of the CCL, namely Rajanikanta Singh to be held on 11th November, 2024.

2. Registered it as JJB/SPT Misc Case no. 14 of 2024.

3. Section 98(1) of Juvenile Justice (Care and Protection of Children) Act, 2015 clearly mentions that:

The Committee or the Board, as the case may be, may permit leave of absence to any child, to allow him, on special occasions like examination, marriage of relatives, death of kith or kin or accident or serious illness of parent or any emergency of like nature, under supervision, for a period generally not exceeding seven days in one instance, excluding the time taken in journey.

4. Considering the above mentioned provision of the Act and the *Principle of non-waiver of rights*, the board is of the opinion to accept the prayer in the Best Interest of the Child.

5. So, the prayer is allowed for five days leave from today, the 8th November 2024 upto 12th November 2024 and the CCL is returnable on 12th November 2024 before 3 p.m.

6. Send a copy to the Superintendent of Observation Home.

7. The Misc. Case is disposed of accordingly.

<table>
<tr><td align="center">(signature)
Member
Juvenile Justice Board
Senapati District</td><td align="center">(signature)
Member
Juvenile Justice Board
Senapati District</td></tr>
</table>

PART 14

Travel Expense of CCLs on Their Attendance Before the Board

Another remarkable order passed by the Board when I was in the JJB Imphal East District on 14th December 2016. That, Learned Advocate Oinam Chittaranjan Singh on behalf of a CCL submitted an application praying for providing travel allowance for the CCL *to and fro* from his home to the Office of the Board. This kind of order for travelling expenses is the first time in history Juvenile Justice movement in the State of Manipur. So, I am reproducing in toto for reference by concealing the identity of the CCL. This order may be considered historical and to be followed by the future members of the Boards. Thus,

Juvenile Justice Board, Imphal East District

Manipur

<u>JJB Misc Case No.3 of 2016</u>

Ref:- FIR Case No.74(09) 2011 HNG/IE P.S.

The State of Manipur

-Vs-

Mr XXXX,

S/o Mr.....

of...............

Heingang PS, Imphal East District, Manipur

<u>ORDER</u>

14th December 2016

The present application is filed by the Counsel for the CCL U/S 91(2) JJ Act 2015 for affording travelling allowance for the CCL and one escort for appearance of the CCL before the Board.

Registered the case as JJB IE Misc Case 3 of 2024.

Section 91(2) of JJ Act 2015 provide as under:-

(2) Where the attendance of a child is required before the Board or the Committee, such child shall be entitled to travel reimbursement for self and one escort accompanying the child as per actual expenditure incurred, by the Board, or the Committee or the District Child Protection Unit, as the case may be.

It is clearly provided under the above mentioned Section that actual travelling expenditure of the CCL along with escort accompanying the CCL has to be reimbursed by the Board unless the appearance the CCL is dispensed under Section 91(1) of the same act.

Hence, prayer for allowing travelling allowance for the CCL is allowed as per provisions mentioned above.

Application is disposed of accordingly.

<table>
<tr><td align="center">***Signed***</td><td align="center">***Signed***</td></tr>
<tr><td align="center">Member</td><td align="center">Principal Magistrate</td></tr>
<tr><td align="center">Juvenile Justice Board</td><td align="center">Juvenile Justice Board</td></tr>
<tr><td align="center">Imphal East</td><td align="center">Imphal East</td></tr>
</table>

PART 15

Sports

Rule no. 53(vii) of JJ Rules 2016 states that in the child care institutes, the provision for the rehabilitation and re-integration of children shall include recreational activities including sports

Before The Juvenile Justice Board
Senapati District, Manipur
<u>JJB Misc Case No. 21 of 2024</u>

Ref. FIR No. 74(9)2024 SPT PS
U/S 64/329 BNS

State

V

Loushambam Sanayanba, aged about 15 years
s/o. Loushambam Jogesh Singh of
Taranithoi Bazar,
PO & PS Senapati, Senapati District, Manipur
Child in Conflict with Law (CCL)

<u>ORDER</u>

03/11/2024

Present:

L. Tomchou, Ld. APP

S.Subash, Ld. Counsel of the CCL

Loushambam Jogesh Singh, father of the CCL

1. The Present petition is filed by Loushambam Jogesh Singh of Taranithoi Bazar,Senapati on behalf of his son Loushambam Sanayanba to grant permission to attend 8(eight) months football coaching at Th. Surchandra Singh Football Academy, Sagolband, Imphal West. Submitted schedule and duration of the training.

2. Register it as JJB Misc Case.

3. The present condition is that the CCL is presently staying at Observation Home, Takyelpat and now pursuing class 1st Semester in Arts.

4. The Ld. Counsel of the CCL submitted the Th. Surchandra Singh Football Academy is at Sagolband, Imphal West. Duration of the training shall be ranged for eight months beginning by 13th November, 2024 up to 12rd July, 2025 in the morning from 6 a.m. to 9 a.m.

5. Loushambam Jogesh Singh, father of the CCL submitted that all the responsibilities of caring and escorting of the CCL shall be borne by him.

6. Considering the right to development of the child under Rule no. 53(vii) JJ Rules 2016, the prayer is allowed on the following conditions:

   1. The CCL is permitted to go to the Academy along with his father. The father of the CCL is directed

to pick up the CCL at 5:00 a.m. and drop him back before 9:00 a.m. of every morning.

2. All the responsibilities of caring and escorting of the CCL should be borne by the Father of the CCL.

7. The Misc.case is disposed of accordingly.

8. Send a copy of this order to Superintendent of the Observation Home and Manager, Th. Surchandra Singh Football Academy, Sagolband, Imphal West.

<table>
<tr><td>(Signature)</td><td>(Signature)</td></tr>
<tr><td>Member</td><td>Member</td></tr>
<tr><td>Juvenile Justice Board</td><td>Juvenile Justice Board</td></tr>
<tr><td>Senapati District</td><td>Senapati District</td></tr>
</table>

PART 16

Initiation of Inquiry

Inquiry shall be started from the time of the first production of a CCL before the Board and shall be completed within a period of four months. If the inquiry is not completed within this period, another two months may be extended.[26] However, the provision of speedy inquiry is enshrined in the Act, the realization of this provision is hardly possible due to many reasons.

Another way of inquiry can be done as per section 173 CrPC or 193 BNSS. Thus, it is the duty of the Board to take cognizance of the offence when the Final Investigation Report (Charge Sheet) is submitted before the Board from the Investigating agency. We may write in such a way as shown below when the Final Investigation Report is received.

Specimen order
Ref.:- FIR No. 209(10)2023 SPT PS
U/S 302 IPC

---

26 Section 14, JJ Act 2015

<u>ORDER</u>

The 4/4/2024

Case is put up today. Final investigation report is filed by the IO stating prima facie case established the commission of offence u/s 302 IPC, Senapati-PS against the CCL.

Perused the record. Find sufficient ground for proceeding against the CCL. Issue summons to the CCL to appear before the Board on 18/4/2024.

(Signature)	(Signature)
Member	Member
Juvenile Justice Board	Juvenile Justice Board
Senapati District	Senapati District

Specimen order of Offence Hearing

Before the Juvenile Justice Board,
Senapati District, Manipur
JJB/SPT Inquiry Case No. 2 of 2023

Ref: FIR No. 209(10)2023 SPT PS

U/S 376 IPC

The State of Manipur

Vs

Narayan Singh, 16 yrs
s/o Harideva Singh
Taranithoi Bazar,
PO & PS Senapati, Senapati District, Manipur
CCL

<u>ORDER</u>

17/7/2024

Present:

Mr. P P Singh, Ld Counsel for the CCL

Kh. Lakhi, Ld. Government Counsel for the State

Narayan Singh CCL

Taoroinai Luwang, Ld. LPO

Mrs. Ibemcha, mother of the CCL

1. The case is fixed for offence explanation. Brief facts leading to the present case is that the present FIR was registered in pursuant to written report filed by the complainant namely RK Tilen s/o (L) RK Radhakumar Singh of Taoroinai bazaar, Senapati, PS-Senapati reported to the OC Senapati PS stating that on 05/10/2023 at about 3:00 p.m, the complainant's granddaughter namely Baby Sonali aged about 4 yrs has been raped by the CCL Namely Narayan Singh inside the building of A.E. office, PWD Senapati Division, Manipur State.

2. Ld. Govt Counsel submitted that there is *prima facie* case for commission of the offence as alleged.

3. Counsel for the CCL on the other hand submitted that the CCL was wrongly charged of sexual assault by the complainant and hence no offence is made out, counsel pray for discharge of the CCL.

4. Perused the materials on record.

5. The offence alleged against the CCL is explained to the CCL. The CCL submits that he was not aware about the offence at the time of incident which occurred more than 17 years back. He further submitted that he is not aware about the offence and submitted that

the offence charged against him and he came to know about the offence very recently.

6. Today itself the CCL is asked to plead guilty or not guilty.

Question: Do you plead guilty?
Answer: No. I do not plead guilty.

7. The opinion of the Board is that the inquiry would be conducted against the CCL whether he committed the offence u/s 376 IPC.

8. So, the Ld APP is directed to produce witnesses.

9. Summon witnesses.

10. Fixed 21 /8/2024 for PW.

<table>
<tr><td align="center">(signature)</td><td align="center">(signature)</td></tr>
<tr><td align="center">Member</td><td align="center">Member</td></tr>
<tr><td align="center">Juvenile Justice Board</td><td align="center">Juvenile Justice Board</td></tr>
<tr><td align="center">Senapati District</td><td align="center">Senapati District</td></tr>
</table>

Specimen Order to produce CCL

Before the Juvenile Justice Board,
Senapati District, Manipur

Ref: FIR No. 209(10)2023 SPT PS
U/S 376/34 IPC

The State of Manipur

Vs

Narayan Singh, 16 yrs
s/o Harideva Singh
Taranithoi Bazar,
PO & PS Senapati, Senapati District, Manipur

...Child in Conflict with law

<u>ORDER</u>
DATE 02/05/2024

The CCL fails to appear before the Board.

Summon is served through process server. But report is not returned till date.

Since the case is of heinous nature. O.C. SPT PS is directed to take necessary step to produce the CCL before the board on 16/5/2024.

Fixed 16/5/2024 for further proceeding.

<table>
<tr><td>(Signature)</td><td>(Signature)</td></tr>
<tr><td>Member</td><td>Member</td></tr>
<tr><td>Juvenile Justice Board</td><td>Juvenile Justice Board</td></tr>
<tr><td>Senapati District</td><td>Senapati District</td></tr>
</table>

Specimen Order to produce CCL (2nd step)

Before the Juvenile Justice Board,
Senapati District, Manipur

Ref: FIR No. 209(10)2023 SPT PS
U/S 376/34 IPC

The State of Manipur

Vs

Narayan Singh, 16 yrs
s/o Harideva Singh
Taranithoi Bazar,
PO & PS Senapati, Senapati District, Manipur

...Child in Conflict with law

<u>ORDER</u>

Date 16/07/2024

Report filed by Th Simon CWPO of SPT PS dated 10/7/2024 is received stating that the CCL was engaged to a duty outside of the State and that there is no chance to serve the notice to the said CCL.

Perused the report received from the SJPO SPT PS, the case record is put up today.

Vide order dated 2/5/2024 the OC, SPT PS was directed to take necessary step to produce the CCL before the Board on 16/7/2024. The similar order was passed by the Board vide order dated 15/6/2024.

In the circumstances, SJPU is directed to apprehend the CCL and produce him on next date

Fix 12/8/2024 for production of the CCL.

<table>
<tr><td>(Signature)</td><td>(Signature)</td></tr>
<tr><td>Member</td><td>Member</td></tr>
<tr><td>Juvenile Justice Board</td><td>Juvenile Justice Board</td></tr>
<tr><td>Imphal East</td><td>Imphal East</td></tr>
</table>

Specimen warrant of apprehending the CCL

Before the Juvenile Justice Board, Senapati District

Address: Old DC Building, Senapati

Form No. 2

WARRANT OF APPREHEND OF CCL

U/s 72 BNSS

Ref: FIR No. 10(3) 2023 SPT PS
U/S 376/34 IPC

To,
Officer-In-Charge
Senapati Police Station, Senapati

Whereas Narayan Singh, 16 yrs s/o Harideva Singh, Taranithoi Bazar, PO & PS Senapati, Senapati District, Manipur stands allegation with the offence of rape upon a woman by breaking open her door in the night of 15/3/2014 along with another person. You are hereby directed to apprehend the said CCL and produce him before the Board on 12/08/2024 at 11:30 a.m.

Dated, the 16 July 2024

(Signature)   (Signature)
Member   Member
Juvenile Justice Board   Juvenile Justice Board
Senapati District   Senapati District

PART 17

Closure Report

When there is no sufficient evidence to proceed against an accused, the police file to the court a report. This report is called closure report. Section 189 BNS read as "If, upon an investigation under this Chapter, it appears to the officer in charge of the police station that there is not sufficient evidence or reasonable ground of suspicion to justify the forwarding of the accused to a Magistrate, such officer shall, if such person is in custody, release him on his executing a bond or bail bond, as such officer may direct, to appear, if and when so required, before a Magistrate empowered to take cognizance of the offence on a police report, and to try the accused or commit him for trial".

Under this section, some steps may be taken up as the following for finalizing of a case after Closure Report (CR) is submitted by the investigating agency:

1. Write order of receiving CR and summon the Complainant and fix a date;
2. Next sitting: Hear the complainant whether they desire to proceed further the case against the CCL or agree with CR.
3. Then, three options may be there (1) if the complainant accepts the CR, then dispose of the

case; (2) if the complainant does not accept the CR or, then give order to the investigating agency for Re-investigating the case; or (3) the Board may continue as it thinks fit.

A specimen Summon to the complainant

Before the Juvenile Justice Board,
Senapati District, Manipur
JJB /SPT Inquiry Case no. 4 of 2024

Ref: 39(7)2023 WPS SPT
U/S 307 IPC

The State of Manipur
Vs
Narayan Singh, 16 yrs
s/o Harideva Singh
Taranithoi Bazar,
PO & PS Senapati, Senapati District, Manipur

To,

Mr Lorii Dikho
S/o. Kavita Dikho
of Mao, Mao-PS.

WHEREAS, your name has been cited as complainant/ Informant in the above referred FIR case.

WHEREAS, on 21/5/2024 at 2:00 p.m. this Board had fixed for your appearance and examination i/c with the aforesaid FIR. Accordingly, you are hereby summoned to appear before this Board on the said date and time so as to enable this Board to proceed further.

Take notice that if you fail to comply with this order without lawful excuse. You will be subjected to consequences of non-attendance.

Given our hand and seal of this Board on this 10 May 2024.

(Signature)
Member
Juvenile Justice Board
Senapati District

(Signature)
Member
Juvenile Justice Board
Senapati District

PART 18

Suo Moto

Suo Moto means the action taken by a court of its own accord, without any request by the parties involved.

The word "cognizance" has no esoteric or mystic significance in criminal law or procedure. It merely means—become aware of and when used with reference to a court or Judge, to take notice of judicially, The court said that 'taking cognizance' does not involve any formal action; or indeed action of any kind, but occurs as soon as a Magistrate, as such applies his mind to the suspected commission of an offence; Fakhruddin Ahmad v. State of Uttaranchal, 2008 AIR SCW 5881: AIR 2009 SC (Supp) 803: (2008) 12 SCALE 339: 2008 Cr LJ 4377 (SC); Ajit Kumar Palit v. State of West Bengal, (1963) Supp 1 SCR 953: AIR 1963 SC 765: (1963) 1 Cr LJ 797: 1964 (1) SCJ 75.[27]

Thus, Suo Moto Cognizance means the action taken by a court without being prompted by another party.

---

27 Fakhruddin Ahmad v. State of Uttaranchal, 2008 AIR SCW 5881: AIR 2009 SC (Supp) 803: (2008) 12 SCALE 339: 2008 Cr LJ 4377 (SC); Ajit Kumar Palit v. State of West Bengal, (1963) Supp 1 SCR 953: AIR 1963 SC 765: (1963) 1 Cr LJ 797: 1964 (1) SCJ 75

As per section 4 (2) of JJ Act 2015, JJB has the powers conferred by the Criminal Procedure Code 1973 now the Bharatiya Nagarik Suraksha Sanhita, 2023 (BNSS).

JJB has the right to initiate a Suo Moto case under section 358 BNSS or 319 CrPC. The Board may take Suo Moto Cognizance against a person who is not being the accused has committed any offence for which such person could be tried together with the accused. Section 358 BNSS reads as:

Section 358 BNSS reads as: (*1*) Where, in the course of any inquiry into, or trial of, an offence, it appears from the evidence that any person not being the accused has committed any offence for which such person could be tried together with the accused, the Court may proceed against such person for the offence which he appears to have committed.

(*2*) Where such person is not attending the Court, he may be arrested or summoned, as the circumstances of the case may require, for the purpose aforesaid.

(*3*) Any person attending the Court, although not under arrest or upon a summons, may be detained by such Court for the purpose of the inquiry into, or trial of, the offence which he appears to have committed.

(*4*) Where the Court proceeds against any person under sub-section (*1*), then—

(*a*) the proceedings in respect of such person shall be commenced afresh, and the witnesses re-heard;

(*b*) subject to the provisions of clause (*a*), the case may proceed as if such person had been an accused person when the Court took cognizance of the offence upon which the inquiry or trial was commenced.

Further, **any Magistrate of the first class may take Suo Moto cognizance** of any offence upon information received from any person other than a police officer, or **upon his own knowledge,** that such offence has been committed under section 210 BNSS or 190 CrPC. Section 210 (1) BNSS is read as:

Section 210 BNSS reads as: 210. (*1*) Subject to the provisions of this Chapter, **any Magistrate of the first class,** and any Magistrate of the second class specially empowered in this behalf under sub-section (2), **may take cognizance of any offence—**

(*a*) upon receiving a complaint of facts, including any complaint filed by a person authorised under any special law, which constitutes such offence;

(*b*) upon a police report (submitted in any mode including electronic mode) of such facts;

(*c*) upon information received from any person other than a police officer, or **upon his own knowledge,** that such offence has been committed.

A Magistrate can take cognizance of any offence either on receiving a complaint of facts which constitute an offence or a police report of such facts or upon receipt of information from any person other than a police officer or upon his own knowledge, that such an offence has been committed; *Shivjee*

Singh v. Nagendra Tiwary, 2010 Cr LJ 3827: AIR 2261: (2010) 6 SCALE 307 (SC).[28]

While expressing the opinion that the magistrate could take cognizance of the offence notwithstanding the contrary opinion of the police the Court observed that the Magistrate could take cognizance under section 190(1)(c).; *H. S. Bains Director... Vs The State (Union Territory of Chandigarh) 1980 AIOR 1883, 1981 SCR (1) 935 (4) SCC 631.*[29]

Some steps of drafting a Suo moto may be summarized as under:

1. Write report of abuse or assault to the child or offence committed by a child;
2. Register it as Suo Moto Case;
3. Give direction to concerned police for investigation;
4. Fixed a date for report.

A specimen sample of Suo Moto

Before the Juvenile Justice Board,
Senapati District, Manipur
U/S 210 BNSS
JJB/SPT/Suo Moto Case 1 of 2024
<u>ORDER</u>
22/5/2024

It is learnt from reliable sources that a girl was bitterly beaten up by a warden in a hostel somewhere in Senapati town. Some viral photos in the social media are also seen.

---

28 Shivjee Singh v. Nagendra Tiwary, 2010 Cr LJ 3827: AIR 2261: (2010) 6 SCALE 307 (SC)

29 H. S. Bains Director... Vs The State (Union Territory of Chandigarh) 1980 AIOR 1883, 1981 SCR (1) 935 (4) SCC 631

Registered it as JJB/SPT Suo Moto Case no.1 of 2024.

O.C. Women PS, Senapati District is directed to investigate the incident and take necessary action

Fixed 6/6/2024 for report.

(Signature)   (Signature)
Member   Member
Juvenile Justice Board   Juvenile Justice Board
Senapati District   Senapati District

Conclusion

In this manual book my humble attempt was to help Juvenile Justice Board (JJB) Members in drafting orders handily and effectively. Based on my own experience, it is my fervent hope that studying and understanding the specimen orders presented here would be quite helpful for the newly appointed members. While few model orders are commonly applicable and crucial ones, these should be kept at fingertips.

Even if a Member is unfamiliar with drafting orders, they can use these specimen orders as a framework by copying and modifying them as needed. That is the main purpose why the specimen orders were inserted in this manual.

Additionally, Members should make an effort to familiarize themselves with some particular sections of Acts and laws, which are indispensable to make an appropriate Order, as highlighted in the introduction of this manual.

If any doubts arise, Members should never hesitate to seek guidance from the Principal Magistrate, Senior Advocates, or the Additional Public Prosecutor.

By following the intents and contents as reflected in specimen orders, Members, in the course of time, would be able to quickly grasp the essential components of drafting.

It is sincerely hoped that this manual book proves helpful for newly appointed Social Worker Members of Juvenile Justice Boards across the country.

....